School's Over

School's Over

How to Have Freedom &
Democracy in Education

Jerry Mintz

School's Over
How to Have Freedom and Democracy in Education

Alternative Education Resource Organization
417 Roslyn Road
Roslyn Heights, NY 11577

Cover: Black Dog Designs
Layout: Isaac Graves

Printed in the United States of America.

Library of Congress Control Number: 2016957549
ISBN: 978-0986016011

To my grandfather, William M. Blatt.
He took the time to ask me when I was a child,
"What do you want to learn?"

I hate this darn unthinking school
Which professes to teach you the Golden Rule—
"You fool me and I'll make you a fool"
Against this I will rebel

Many's the time when I've hated to stay
When the bored, boring teacher had nothing to say.
But "No!" says the teacher, "You can't go away!"
And this I will also retell

So I learned what the bored, boring teacher had taught
And, thusly, I learned to be bored on the spot.
And ever since, I've been bored at the thought
Of the trash that the school has to sell

Oh, I'm sure education in school's not all bad
And I'll know things of interest when I am a grad.
But the camouflage job on the interest is sad
And the learning won't set very well

And so every morning at just 8 o'clock
I rush in the school and behind me they lock
The door to my prison, and I start to walk
Through the prison, from cell to cell.

A poem by Jerry Mintz,
written when he was a 15-year-old high school student.

Contents

Foreword
Sir Ken Robinson

This book is about democratic schools and how and why they are radically different from conventional schools. In fully democratic schools, students have executive powers in the governance of their own learning and in all the decisions that affect it, including how the school is run, the schedule, curriculum, assessment, facilities, and even the hiring of faculty. Democratic schools may seem the polar opposite of the adult-directed and custodial nature of much of conventional education. In many ways they are. And yet, they are the practical embodiment of principles that school systems everywhere typically proclaim: the need to develop independent learners, to cultivate diverse talents, to produce thoughtful, compassionate, and productive citizens. So why and how are democratic schools so different from regular ones? Let me highlight some core themes.

The first is that learning is a natural process. Human beings are intensely curious organisms and children are endlessly interested in the world around them. They love to learn and want to learn. It's a sad irony that so many of them seem to lose interest in learning as they make their way through regular schools. Too many become bored and stressed by the whole process. One reason is that the rituals of conventional schooling often contradict the rhythms of natural learning. Democratic schools aim to resonate with those rhythms and in doing so to nourish children's natural appetite for learning. That has implications for the curriculum and who shapes it, for teaching and who does it, and for the schedule and who decides it.

A second theme is that learning is largely a social process. Learning is a personal accomplishment but children learn hugely from those around them. Take language. Young children readily absorb the spoken language (or languages) of the people they're most exposed to, and the local dialect and accents too. It would create a stir if a child who's raised in an exclusively Italian or Russian-speaking community suddenly started to speak Inuit or Gaelic. So-called feral children, who grow up away from human culture, may never learn to speak at all. If they're raised by apes or dogs they may growl or bark, but they don't speak in complex sentences and slip into the subjunctive. In learning to speak, children also absorb the values, beliefs, and behaviors of their communities. Consequently, although the impulse to learn is natural, much of what we do learn is cultural.

In conventional schools, children are taught and assessed as individuals, often on the basis of competitive grading systems. They are taught *in* groups but not *as* groups. Democratic schools are inherently social institutions, which facilitate a deep sense of community, of collaborative learning and collective responsibility. That has implications for the overall culture of the school.

A third theme is a firm belief in the rights and abilities of young people to make decisions about their own lives and the conditions of their own education. In conventional schools, the main decisions are taken by adults and the students follow the program. They may have some options along the way but the path is pretty well staked out in advance, irrespective of the young people who are obliged to take it. Democratic schools operate on the principle that if they are trusted and entrusted, young people are capable of fine judgments in matters that affect their education and are entitled to make them. That has implications for structures of responsibility and for who decides what and for whom.

Jerry Mintz is uniquely well placed to write this book. He has unparalleled experience of democratic education in all sorts of settings around the world. Under his direction, AERO, the Alternative Education Resource Organization, has become the principal resource for parents, students, and educators everywhere who are looking for or practicing alternative forms of education. His book is part reportage, part memoir, and part manifesto for thinking differently about our children and acting differently in their education.

In a recent interview about the industrial origins of mass education, I was asked, "If schools used to be the answer, what's the answer now?" I think schools are still the answer, just not the schools we've become used to. As mass education has evolved over the past two hundred years or so, we've come to think of schools as particular sorts of institution with distinctive characteristics: classrooms with desks, age related year groups, subject divisions and hierarchies, tests and examinations, remedial groups, and exclusions. But most features of regular schools are shaped by management habits not principles of learning. Properly conceived a school is just a community of people that comes together to learn with and from each other. Schools can exist anywhere and be organized in myriad ways to suit their purposes. Democratic schools are rooted in the purposes of democracy itself: liberty and the pursuit of happiness, self-determination, and government by and for the people. The core message of this book is that if we're serious about these principles in society, we should do more than preach them in education; we should practice them in our schools.

Jerry Mintz is well aware of the skepticism that these alternative approaches can provoke. Democratic schools may be fine for the well-heeled middle classes or for those in small private schools, but what about at-risk children in large public schools in poor neighborhoods? It may be OK to involve older children in some marginal decisions in school, but surely not very young ones in decisions that really matter? Isn't handing the governance of schools to students a recipe for anarchy or self-indulgence, a soft option for educators, and a dereliction of duty by parents? These all sound like common sense objections. Like a lot of common sense, they are mistaken.

This book shows that democratic education works for all ages, in all settings. So far from being a soft option, it is more not less demanding of schools. It depends on shared respect for individuals and empathy for the needs of the group. It depends on the commitment of the whole community to a sense of common purpose and mutual wellbeing. These values are, after all, what democracy is about. And, as you're about to find out, when practiced properly in schools, democracy actually works.

Sir Ken Robinson
Los Angeles, October 2016

Chapter One

The Magic of Democracy

At its core, democracy should mean something very specific: the empowerment of a group of people to make real decisions about their lives. It should describe the process in which people have the ability to debate and discuss and take action based on the conclusion of the community at hand.

In a school setting, democracy is problematic because there are still compulsory school laws. This means that no matter how democratic a school is, an element of choice is absent; children are required to be in some kind of educational program. Often the assumption is that students in a democratic school are there because they want to be in that school as opposed to any other, but that doesn't necessarily mean that they wouldn't rather be somewhere else.

Given that caveat, democracy in a school works the same way it would anywhere: when there is a decision to be made, the people of the school gather to make it. Democracy in schools also works on the small scale: when an individual seeks to make a decision—about how they spend their time, or what action they should take in a particular situation—they are empowered to do so within the boundaries they've helped to establish as a part of the whole community.

In this discussion of democratic power in the hands of children, I am making an assumption I should put on the table right away. People are natural learners. Children are natural learners. They don't need to be "motivated" to learn. We have no way of predicting what kinds of things each one of us is going to want to learn or do, and in fact, the words "learn" and "do" pretty much blur together—learning isn't in some separate compartment. Even when people are being forced to study something, you can never tell exactly what they're learning; is it the subject matter or how to pass a test? Are they mastering the material or the responses an instructor is looking for? Similarly, although we can make guesses about *when* people are learning, it is such a highly personal, individual experience that it can be hard to nail down. Some people have an outward display of an "aha!" moment, others have an internal click that is harder to see.

Children who are part of a democratic school, and participate in a democratic meeting, have the chance to tap into a source of energy and creativity that is not accessed in an ordinary school. People often use words like "spontaneity" and "creativity" when describing children, but you don't truly see those qualities in action until you're in a learning situation where anything is possible, where the children aren't always being told what to do.

When I talk to children about the idea behind this kind of school, it usually takes mere seconds for them to inherently understand. I was once in an elevator when a woman asked me what the "Education Revolution" printed on my shirt meant. As I launched into a philosophical answer, her 9-year-old son interrupted to keep me on track. "Yes," he said, "but what do you really do?" "You get to decide what your school rules are democratically," I said, "And you don't have to go to classes unless you want to." Without hesitating he responded, "Sign me up!"

It's amazing how consistent this response is, and equally amazing that—while a clear indication that children know what they want—so few adults will even acknowledge this reaction as meaningful. There exists in our culture an infuriating acceptance of children's dislike of school, of their unhappiness. It seems almost like a joke when adults chuckle and shrug, "Of course they don't want to go to classes!" The unspoken assumption, counter to one I've made above, is that they are indolent, unfocused, unable to make decisions that serve their minds and bodies.

The prevalence of this notion exists in spite of modern research that continues to prove that the brain is aggressive and ready to learn, that children are natural scientists, observing and cataloguing and quickly understanding the world around them. So, as study after study refutes the idea that children are lazy, what if we all stopped to look at school from another angle? Maybe the problem doesn't lie within the hundreds of thousands of discontented children; maybe the problem is inherent to the one, overarching system meant, somehow, to serve them all.

*****

It is hard to fight against the inertia of our huge

education system, this multi-trillion dollar system that wants to maintain its own shape. In many ways the public school, or the educational bureaucracy, is like a giant balloon. There could be an innovation that begins at some point on the surface and starts pushing in and changing the shape of the balloon. You may even be able to push all the way through, to touch the other side, but as soon as that innovation stops or that innovator goes away, the pressure comes off and the balloon goes back to its original shape. Attempting to shift momentum internally, at this point in time, can only go so far. Alternatives and options outside of this system, then, are becoming increasingly important, especially as layers of bureaucracy build up over the years, ossifying a system that was rigid to begin with.

It is not easy, though, to make a leap of faith and trust children with power over their own lives, especially having not experienced it yourself. One of the main things I recommend to potential teachers and parents is to see a democratic school, or meeting, in operation. I have an incredibly hard time communicating the importance—and dynamism—of democracy, but each time I've visited a school or conference or gathering to give a demonstration of democratic process, within five or ten minutes it takes on a life of its own and the innate potential is on display. You can feel the power of it as soon as people discover that they're talking about real and significant things and are in a position to make real and significant decisions. They are emboldened by their own strength, by the meaning possible in working directly with a group of others to shape their world.

Once adults have seen this, it can become easier, at least on an intellectual level, to acknowledge the function and purpose of democratic education. For many adults, though, being in relationship with students in a democratic setting (whether as a parent or teacher) highlights the fear and uncertainty born of experience in a compulsory setting.

When people haven't experienced freedom they are often afraid of what they might do if they had freedom. Perhaps there is anger that has built up over a period of time, perhaps there is doubt in oneself; the compulsory school system, as it exists now, encourages people to be dependent on others for decision making. It is a system built on disempowerment, and thus, relying on yourself to make decisions, to direct your own time and energy, is an unknown. It's scary. And if adults haven't come through to the other side of these feelings, it can be hard to believe that children have the ability to live in freedom.

The necessity of democratic schools, then, extends beyond the well-being of the children to the parents and teachers as well. For adults who are coming to democratic schools for the first time, it is important to begin with an intellectual understanding, to acknowledge their anxiety and unfounded attachment to the idea that children aren't learning—that they won't learn—unless they're made to, and to choose, in spite of those feelings, to trust children. In taking these steps, adults, too, have an equally incredible opportunity to learn and grow and, alongside their children, change the shape of education.

Chapter Two
The Power of Democracy

D emocratic schools empower children, solidifying their self-confidence, autonomy, identity, and at the core of this experience is the democratic meeting. Each school has a different kind of meeting, but perhaps most important in each, is to define what decisions the meeting has the power to make. Democracy can't be faked. Children absolutely know when they're being given real power and when they aren't.

This is one reason why democracy in a school can be a fragile thing. If adults are willing to overturn or ignore a decision, the credibility of the meeting crumbles; trust in the process is broken; suspicion in adults can grow and the investment of the students can wane. It's very important, then, that the parameters of power are set and understood from the start. Some schools give their students the power to influence budgetary and hiring decisions; some schools retain the adult right to veto decisions based on health and safety, but no matter how large or small the sphere of power, it is critical that it is never thwarted, co-opted, or counteracted.

People have often asked me, "How can we do a meeting in a single classroom or in the family?" Very simply, you start out by saying to the children involved, "These are the areas in which we can't empower you and these are the areas in which we can," and then be consistent—stick to what you've said. If you do that, holding democratic meetings can be useful in almost any situation.

For example, many years ago I volunteered at the local recreation center teaching table tennis. I was only there two days a week for a couple of hours each day, but the club was open six days a week. At first, I taught children 13-years-old and older, but often they would lose interest, so I came when I had time and didn't keep a set schedule. When I started teaching the younger children, though, there was so much interest that I had to commit myself to a real schedule for the first time.

Eventually I realized that the way to keep things properly organized would be to let decisions about the rules be made at a democratic meeting that we'd operate specifically for people involved in the Table Tennis Club. The plan was that some of the children could be elected as leaders or supervisors by the meeting.

This would seem to be a very limited area: we're talking about a recreation center that basically ran as an authoritarian organization—adult staff members had the power to make decisions, without input from the community, that affected everyone involved—and yet, the Table Tennis Club became a powerful program because of democracy.

There was a healthy diversity to the group, both in socio-economic and racial backgrounds, and as the children realized that each of their decisions had been implemented, without exception, the meetings became increasingly complex, tackling more and more serious philosophical questions. Even though they spent their days in regular public school classrooms, the children had total faith in the meeting.

The group created a challenge ladder with 30 or 40 children on it. A couple of early controversies swirled around the boy who was one of the higher players on the ladder. In one situation, he let his cousin beat him and then he beat his cousin to bring his cousin up on the ladder. This was discussed at a meeting I'll never forget, because I've never been in another one like it.

We started out discussing the ethics of whether somebody should be allowed to do this, to organize to let someone beat him or her, and then beat the person back. At the start of the meeting, we were in a separate room, but we had to vacate the room halfway through and were forced to go out to the main room with all kinds of noise and chaos around us. The children put seats in a circle and even though they had to yell to be heard, they would not leave the meeting until a decision had been made.

The group decided to make a rule against this activity, but that in this case there would be no consequence for the boy who did it because there had been no rule about it. From then on, if you broke this rule and let someone beat you on purpose, you would go to the bottom of the ladder. The children took the situation seriously. They were committed to finding agreement—no matter how long it took or how challenging the physical setting—and came to a decision that was deemed fair and equitable by all parties.

I once had discussion with one of the staff members of the center who shared that he had noticed really profound changes in some of the children who, before becoming involved in the Table Tennis Club, had been pretty much out of control. Many of the children I worked with had been labeled "difficult" by adults who worked with them in other settings. I didn't know this, which is the way I prefer to enter into relationships with children; no baggage, high expectations.

These "difficult" children thrived. They were elected to positions like assistant supervisor or supervisor for the Table Tennis Club. They came to realize that in this situation their peers were the authority figures, *they* were the authority figures, and that listening to the group, adjusting behavior when necessary, was the clearest way to meet their personal goals.

One student in particular, one of these "problem" children, was elected assistant supervisor even though people knew all along that he harbored some bad habits. He was cheating, they said, and taunting people and putting them down. One day several different children made complaints about him. At the next meeting he was put on the agenda to be talked about, but the children did not vote him out as assistant supervisor. The meeting served to give him feedback, letting him know that he couldn't behave like that if he wanted to keep his position. The other children knew he really loved it.

To me, this meeting—and my experience with the Table Tennis Club on the whole—was a wonderful example of how democracy can function well, lifting up its participants. The children made decisions that were never vetoed or undermined by the staff; if there was something outside the realm of what they had the ability to decide, the adults were upfront about it and the children were accepting. They worked together to solve problems and, as is the case with the boy mentioned above, showed one another compassion and understanding. When given power, children can be the example of how to treat others in a way that's effective, caring, and in which people are receptive to change.

*****

Many schools try to police problems of behavior by guessing what rules they will need to keep everybody under some kind of control. This model has obvious limitations, but one stands out to me: sometimes they just don't guess right because they don't have everybody's input.

One of the things significantly different about democratic schools is that instead of having one authority figure you have the authority of everybody—all of the children, all of the adults. This has a powerful impact on students, particularly ones who are prone to be labeled "difficult," "defiant," or some other variation that hints at their non-conformity.

A rebellious child is often just trying not to lose his or her own identity. Sometimes they pour so much of their energy into fighting authority figures that they almost can't hear what the authority figures are saying to them, they just know they don't want to accept it because it's coming from the "enemy." Thus, the community of a democratic school—in which authority is shared equally and teachers have more time, space, and capacity to recognize the individuality of each student—can be transformative for students who have struggled in other settings.

Unfortunately, once children who have spent the majority their time in traditional schools get to a certain age, the transition to a democratic community can be onerous. Children who have been disempowered for so long can have a shaky sense of who they are outside of the labels they've been given—children who were known as trouble-makers can enter a democratic setting ready to be disruptive; children who have been teachers'-pets can sign up for a plethora of classes without being in touch with what they really want. For these students, what they need most, and what can prove their biggest obstacle, is time.

All children entering an alternative setting need time to adjust, and each students' pace of acclimation is different. Upon becoming part of a democratic environment, new students learn the rhythm of daily life, the format and function of meetings, that adults can be trusted, that *they* are trusted, and that they are responsible for their actions and held accountable, not to some principal in a separate office, but to the community as a whole.

This process, and its necessity in students' experience, is one reason why some schools don't take children over 13-years-old, unless they've already had some kind of experience in alternative education. The longer a person has experienced disempowerment and the abuse of an authoritarian system, the longer they've had their own personality scraped away from them, the longer it's going to take to recover.

While there have been many examples of teenaged students thriving after joining a democratic school, there are also plenty of cases that didn't work out, situations where the internal damage these students carried couldn't be repaired. Each school has to consider not only the situation of a potential student, but each student already attending and the community at large.

In the 1960s, I was interning at Lewis-Wadhams School, which was based on Summerhill. I met and invited a couple of children from nearby who were interested in the school; they spent some time at the school and were interviewed by the principal, Herb Snitzer. One brother was 16 and the other was 12 or 13. Herb was willing to consider the younger brother, but for the 16-year-old he suggested that he just go to college, rather than enter a situation that could open up a lot of interpersonal and emotional work that might take many years to resolve. Beginning college would give him agency and a certain measure of autonomy not present in traditional high school, and the internal work would present itself in other situations. The boy went ahead and did that.

*****

Conversely, the vast majority of students entering an authoritarian system from a democratic school can handle it just fine. This is because when children are constantly having to make decisions, they begin to know who they are, and to know how they feel about almost everything. When these children go into an authoritarian situation, particularly if it's for a limited period of time, they do not feel threatened about losing their identity; they see the situation, instead, as a game that has to be played. They're not worried about losing themselves in that process. I've had students who came back from being in public school who said to me, "Wow, it's so easy. All you have to do is what they tell you to do."

Sometimes it was almost embarrassing because we had children who would not only go on and do well in traditional schools but would also go on to do well in the Army. I thought, "What are we doing? Training children for authoritarian systems?" But these children knew who they were, were in touch with their strengths, and could use authoritarian systems for their own purposes.

Chapter Three
Democratic Community

What makes democratic communities dynamic is that a much higher degree of authority is involved in the decisions that are made. Instead of having one person making administrative decisions, you multiply that by all the other people participating in the community, and there is that much more authority, cooperation, and agreement behind the decisions. This is why democratic schools are able to be so self-disciplined, because so many people are invested in the outcome.

The key responsibility of students in a democratic school is that they have to be prepared to be fully-functioning members of their community. When they decide to join the community, they have to be willing not only to consider their own needs, but the needs of the community as well.

Student leadership is one of the best markers in how functional a school community is. Obviously, students will outnumber staff, and as we've discussed, peer accountability is paramount in a setting where each person holds equal power and authority within the community. If you have students who have been around for a long time and have seen the results of sweeping things under the rug, they understand that it's important to confront things, discuss them, and work together to solve problems that arise.

If too many students within the community do not trust the democratic process, or if they're afraid to confront each other—because as a subgroup they want to support each other—then the democratic system tends to break down. Belief in democracy can be a delicate thing.

Peer pressure and conformity can happen anywhere, all of this ebbs and flows, but generally speaking, peer pressure from cliques is less likely to happen in a democratic school. Hopefully, too, you've got enough people in the community who are not going to be affected by others having a strong opinion about something. In my experience, there are always children who are willing to express an opinion about things they disagree with, even if they are a minority of one!

In some communities, however, there can be pressure (even if it's unintentional) against this kind of speaking up. This is one reason why I tend to distrust consensus decision making: it can make people feel like they don't want to rock the boat, like they don't want to be the one that blocks a decision, and that might prevent them from giving an opinion that's just as valid and thoughtful.

No matter their form, though, democratic meetings teach communication skills. In a meeting structure you must stop and let the other person speak without interrupting her. That changes the nature of the relationship between people, particularly when it comes to adults, who can dominate with the loudness of their voice or by interrupting.

Students also learn how to communicate with a

variety of people, and through these relationships, build respect. Diversity within the community is important because throughout life, people are presented with situations in which they must communicate with people who are from different cultural, ethnic, financial, and experiential backgrounds. The ability to converse and negotiate, to listen to another's point of view, is greatly enhanced by growing up in or being a part of a democratic community.

A.S. Neill, in *Summerhill*, introduced the idea of "freedom, not license." It's a good concept. The difference between freedom and license is to be found in the world of social interaction. You have the freedom to do what you wish up to the point at which you're interfering with somebody else's freedom. When that interference happens, some kind of negotiation needs to take place on an individual basis or in a democratic meeting. If you do something you want to do, but end up trampling over somebody else's ability to do what he wanted to do, that's license, not freedom. Playing music loudly in the middle of the night because you're staying up late and like the sound of it would be considered license if you end up keeping other people awake. On the other hand, if everyone else is on vacation and you're the only one there, it's freedom!

Unfortunately, no particular action can be described as freedom or license in all cases. You have to look at the particular circumstance to make a judgment. This is the nuance of consideration asked of each member of a democratic community. In taking each situation as it comes, hearing multiple perspectives and evaluating a host of outcomes, students are developing empathy, creative problem solving, and critical thinking. When each person is allowed personal freedom, and actively participating in the discussions that arise, freedom is a kind of homeostasis. License, however, is when people act as they want without regard for others. This creates imbalance.

Student leadership, therefore, must not only exist within meetings, but throughout the daily life of the school. All schools eventually establish their own culture, having their own quirks and specific rules based on who is a part of that community. For new students, their experience and understanding of the school is often shaped much more by their fellow students than by the adults. Students who are willing to speak up to correct an infraction of the rules, explain a school tradition, or guide someone through their first meeting are often able do so in a way that is more meaningful than if it were coming from an adult. Everyone is learning in a democratic school, and everyone is a teacher.

Schools with high turnover rates, or that aren't discerning in their admissions processes, can be their own worst enemy when it comes to upholding the culture of their school. Bringing on large groups of new children who haven't had experience with the democratic process, who have been disempowered and carry with them difficult previous experiences with authoritarian schools, can throw a school community into trying times. Adults and longtime students can become overwhelmed and frustrated with the energy it takes to teach a large group of people—who each carry their own baggage—what it means to be in a democratic school. Students who normally speak up and provide leadership can become disengaged, adults may be more prone to focus on damage control, and the care that each individual normally feels can wane. In short, the culture can shift.

*****

Adults who participate in democratic schools must also navigate a unique role. For staff members, it's often a balancing act. While grown ups have certainly had experiences that could be useful for children to know about, it is up to each staff member to work out how to communicate those experiences effectively, how to establish what their role in the school is meant to be. Transparency is the ultimate tool in this task. Students who are able to see what kind of structures adults have made in their own lives, what kinds of skills they've developed, experiences they've had, and the mistakes that they've made, are often more willing to build open, trusting relationships with adults. Those relationships then enable students to decide what advice they might seek, what skills *they* may want to develop, and to be accepting and forgiving of their own mistakes along the way. Staff members are prime resources in a democratic school, and should demonstrate, by the way they interact in the community, effective ways to solve problems, handle crises, and deal with other people fairly and kindly.

The most important role for adults is to help children get better at answering their own questions and meeting their own needs. Not surprisingly, it can be very difficult to find adults who are able to fill this role. The widely accepted dynamic between adults and children is that children are the beneficiaries of adult knowledge—they are asked to accept, unquestioned, what adults present to them. For adults who have had experience in democratic education, stepping out of this dynamic can be intuitive; for those who haven't, it can be learned; for all adults, it is a constant practice.

Academic non-coercion is essential to teacher-student relationships in a democratic school. Students' ability to choose whether or not they go to a class is not only an important expression of students' free will, it diffuses arbitrary power dynamics and provides valuable feedback for teachers. If a teacher has something they deem valuable to share with students, they will need to figure out how to offer it in a way that students want to engage. In democratic settings, teachers have the ability to try many different methods and formats for teaching, as well as chatting directly with students about their needs, learning styles, and interest levels. This process is a key aspect of effective teacher-education. Teachers in traditional schools, because the students are forced to be there and the teachers have a monopoly, might never get this training or feedback throughout a long career.

*****

Parents' roles can vary according to how a school is set up. For examples, if the school is a parent cooperative, they have a big role. Many schools have mandatory volunteer hours, ensuring that parents are participating to one degree or another. For most democratic schools, however,

I believe it's very important that the parents, as much as possible and with minimal interference, allow students and staff to make the decisions about the school. This doesn't mean that parents shouldn't be welcome to spend time in the school, but that when it comes to matters of daily life, parents allow students and staff to take the lead.

Sometimes, parents find themselves in the position of living vicariously through their children's experience at a democratic school. Not only are they excited for their children to participate, but they, too, want to be able to take part in something that most of them never had the opportunity to when they were in school. Just as it's very important to be clear about what kinds of power students have in decision-making, it's just as necessary to establish what kind of forum parents have to be involved. Some schools have parent groups that have control of their own meetings and activities; others have committees that support the school's infrastructure that parents can be a part of; still others provide monthly gatherings where parents can trade ideas and stories and support for one another.

Sadly, there are cases when students are removed from schools when the problem actually lies with their parents. The reasons for removal vary: a parent is dissatisfied with the lack of academic work a student is pursuing, uncomfortable with a conflict their child has with another student, frustrated by an interaction with a staff member. Many schools have avenues for parents to address these kinds of issues, but often the truth is that parents aren't prepared to deal with the internal work *they* must do while having students in an alternative setting. Trusting children with the agency that democratic schools encourage in students can give rise to fear and anxiety—not to mention ridicule from the outside world.

While schools can do their best in supporting parents, and provide a forum for them to support each other, staff also need to be prepared to identify when it is time to part ways with a family. This can be especially difficult if the cause of the split is the parent and not the child, but just as important. If a parent is being disruptive to the school's process—or hindering their child's growth and participation—the relationship will likely crumble eventually and it is better to end it rather than dragging it out.

Ultimately, the biggest role parents have in a democratic school is to support their children by educating themselves on the philosophy and meeting their child's experience with an open mind. Questions will arise, concerns will develop, and each of these moments demand not a knee-jerk reaction, but a careful examination of their root cause. The most successful schools have students who are empowered by each other, their teachers, and their parents.

Chapter Four
How to Run a Meeting

Some people say that democratic meetings can't work in relatively large groups. I've found that it's fine to have a large democratic school as long as you have good communication and a way to get everybody involved in the meetings. To start, it's important to have a comfortable room that's big enough to contain everybody—this can be the limiting factor in a school—and meetings should be hosted in the same place every time.

Everyone who has an opinion should be able to express it. However, it is up to the chairperson if he or she feels someone has been talking too much to point that out to the person, or simply to call on others to get a more balanced discussion going. Being a good chairperson is a learned skill.

There is a pervasive worry that adults have more natural authority, so that children will just blindly listen and follow them. At most democratic schools, this is not an issue; while a new student might be more influenced by an adult voice, in general, students are well practiced in looking at the situation and facts objectively. On the other hand, some adults are respected because they have a good track record and the community finds their contributions useful and believable.

An important opportunity students have in a democratic school is being able to constructively criticize their friends in a meeting; perhaps a friend has broken a rule, mistreated someone, or expressed an opinion that they disagree with. This is an important point of maturity not only for the school, but for the student, because it speaks to the strength of students' relationships and the safety of the meeting. When there is trust that differing opinions won't damage friendships, more ideas are brought to the community, creativity grows, and compromise can bloom.

At many democratic schools—Summerhill is one of them—the director and the staff have the ultimate say in certain areas of decision-making: mainly, health and safety. At these schools, and most others, the community is still sensible enough that whatever situation is brought up, students can work well with staff members and make good decisions about these key areas.

For example, at one democratic boarding school, when it came to the question of drug rules, the children understood that one of the most important things to the school was its public persona, its reputation. They knew this was directly related to how successful they would be in fundraising (crucial to any school) and getting support. Therefore, they felt it was imperative that the school not have the reputation of being full of druggies. They eventually passed a rule, which I have never heard of as being part of any other school, which stated that even day school students had a 24-hour responsibility to the school as long as they wanted to be part of the school community. This meant that if a day student did something that reflected badly on the school, even when they were on their own time, this could be brought up at a school meeting. I don't think any adult would have even considered such a rule, but this was something that came primarily from the students because they felt it was so important.

Most schools based on Sudbury Valley School deal with infractions of rules with something called a Judicial Committee. This committee consists of rotating or elected students and staff members, whose task is to make a judgment and decide an outcome. At many other democratic schools, if an issue comes up that people think would be difficult for the parties involved to talk about in a meeting, or if the meeting feels that more in depth discussion is necessary, they often propose that a "small group" is created. It consists of volunteers who want to work with the person or persons involved in that issue. If it is an interpersonal conflict it should be people who are acceptable to the parties involved. Then, if necessary, the small group can come up with proposals to make to the meeting or simply resolve the situation.

*****

Beyond space, facilitation and record-keeping are crucial to well-functioning meetings. Many schools use a blank, bound volume as a logbook, and don't hold meetings until someone has volunteered to scribe. There are a vast number of decisions made in democratic schools, and sometimes rules are implemented for a recurring issue that becomes moot overtime. It is important, then, to be able to look at what the community has agreed on, and what rule might be ready to be retired. It's so interesting, too, to be able to see what ongoing struggles a group deals with and what proposals do and do not pass; it's such a unique way to observe a community's process!

The chairperson of a democratic meeting needs to have the reflexes of an athlete. They need to know how to listen and how to keep order among participants; they need to be able to summarize people's points and resist the urge to dominate a conversation. They must call on people quickly to keep conversation moving, while also holding an awareness of the order in which people have requested to speak. Sometimes, this awareness is kept through a list—as people raise their hands, their names are added—but personally, I think it's better if the chairperson has more leeway. For example, they should be able to pick somebody who hasn't spoken yet, rather than let the same few people keep on going back and forth. While it can sound harsh, they also need to be firm in keeping the group on topic and should not be hesitant in stopping people immediately to say, "Okay, this is not the subject we're talking about, but if you want we can add it to the agenda."

Some schools run their meetings with the agenda decided in advance, others make it up right there. I believe you should have a combination. If people have something that they need to discuss, it is helpful for it to be put on the agenda in advance so others can know and think about it. On the other hand, I don't think it's right for people to have to wait too long to have something that they want to talk about come up. Some say you can't add to the agenda once it's set; I disagree. If you have a community that has the will to make the best right decision about every subject that comes up, you can get through them fast enough.

*****

The many schools that have been established on the Sudbury Valley model use a set system in communication and decision-making in meetings: the well-established Robert's Rules of Order. Other schools evolve their our own system. My school, Shaker Mountain, was largely influenced by our interaction and early communication with the Lewis-Wadhams School and, later, the Iroquois Confederacy, particularly the Mohawk Tribe.

One of the greatest influences on me was working in the '60s at Lewis-Wadhams School, which was based on Summerhill in England. In Summerhill meetings, for example, they are allowed to have proposals against other proposals. Very often they'll have two or three proposals against each other. And sometimes they'll do "all against all" which means that if the majority of people are against all the proposals, nothing passes. If two proposals could legitimately be against each other, you can have them both on there. If they are not necessarily related to each other directly, so that they could stand alone, you could have several different proposals at a time and vote on them all at once, one at a time, rather than wait, as Robert's Rules says, for the next item to come up.

Personally, I think it's important that meetings be well structured and that they follow the structure consistently. Whatever structure is decided on, whatever has evolved, people need to be well versed in it. For democracy to function and flourish, the meeting must be taken seriously. Everyone should be able to hear whoever is speaking, which requires that everyone show respect and remain quiet if they do not hold the floor. One thing I find useful when I demonstrate meetings with a very large group of students is a portable microphone so that even those with soft voices could be heard.

The way Summerhill controls noise is that the chairperson has the power to warn people and to fine them or kick them out of the meeting if they're being disruptive. At some schools the chairperson gives warnings and if necessary, a noisy person is asked to leave the meeting for a certain period of time. Then they could come back later if they choose.

At one Sudbury School I visited, there was a meeting in which two young students were being very disruptive and were eventually made to leave the meeting. This was later brought to a Judicial Committee meeting that I sat in on. It was decided that the two 5-year-olds would be banned from the next two meetings. When they brought one of them in and told them of their decision he was very happy about it! Later I asked him, "Why don't you just say that you just can't understand what is being discussed in the meeting?" He replied, "I could. But it wouldn't be true. I just find them boring!"

Many democratic schools want to run everything through the regular meeting, using small groups when necessary. It's up to each organization or each school to decide how it wants to deal with these things. Some communities don't want to spend a lot of time dealing with petty disputes between people, or rather, with disputes they consider to be petty. On the other hand, some people think it's important to understand what the community feels about whatever is going on, positive or negative.

Sometimes a child can benefit greatly from just sitting in a meeting and listening. One of the things that disturbs me about some big democratic schools is that such a small percentage of children actually go to the meetings. They can say, "Yes, we're a democracy and people have the right to go to meetings." But it seems to me that if a school is so big that only a minority of the children can get into the meetings, that school is too big.

Participation in meetings can be tricky. Generally, I do not believe in mandatory meetings. At many democratic schools meetings are not mandatory; at some they are. Each school must decide for itself how to encourage engagement in the democratic process. One school came up with an innovative solution: if an issue came up that was deemed important enough that everyone in the school needed to be in on a decision, or to be aware of a particular situation, somebody could propose that the meeting become a "super meeting." If the proposal passed, everybody who was in the school building needed to come to the meeting until it was voted that it was no longer a super meeting. Often, these issues were about health or safety.

*****

In our early years in Shaker Mountain, through our involvement with the Iroquois, we discovered an alternative to the usual "tyranny of the majority." We learned from the Iroquois that it was important to honor the minority. Following a vote, we would poll the minority and if they wished to say something more, they could express their reasons for voting the way they did. Then either they or anybody else in the school community could call for a revote. A re-vote meant that discussion was opened again, making it possible for a new proposal in place of the original one or one proposed against it. We found that this process was more thorough and that when we made a decision we were usually confident that we would not have to come back and revisit the subject.

In my own experiences, I've found consensus-based decision making to be manipulative, often preventing minority opinions from being expressed. Similarly, in a pure majority rules process, you don't often hear what those in the minority have in mind. While people may say, "they had the chance to speak during discussion," the process doesn't lend itself to ensuring every voice is heard. A vote can be taken without each person feeling they had the room to state their opinion.

The Iroquois democratic process uses the best aspects of majority rule and consensus. An ideal decision is made with most people on board, but in the end, it's okay if a decision is made by 25 votes to 23. If nobody in the 23 felt they needed further discussion or a to call for a revote, then what it really meant was that those 23 were doing what the Quakers call "standing aside." They are expressing that they can live with the majority's decision and don't feel the need to continue the discussion. It also means that the minority doesn't have to pretend that they agree with everybody. They could even eventually say, "I told you so," if whatever the majority had decided didn't work out well.

The Iroquois process does take longer than the usual democratic meeting. Giving people who are unhappy with a vote the chance to express their disagreement, or to bring up a facet of the situation that hasn't been considered, inevitably leads to more conversation. For some communities, this longer process is preferable. For others, quick decisions that can later be quickly reversed or revised are favored. Either way, the meeting process is perhaps the most important educational process that happens in a school.

Chapter Five
Iroquois Democracy

1968 was a year in which many new movements were born. I had just started Shaker Mountain and we had four students. One day we all listened to a song recorded by Native American folk singer Buffy St. Marie, called, "My Country, Tis of Thy People You're Dying." It was the story of Native Americans in the United States, but it was not the history of the Native Americans with which most of us were familiar. We wondered if it could really be true—that the white Europeans had so mistreated the natives of this continent.

Our awareness grew as one evening on the news we saw that a group of Mohawk Indians had blockaded a bridge that linked the portion of their reservation located in Upstate New York with the portion located in Canada. They were angry over being charged taxes to go from one part of their land to another.

Not long after that we came in contact with a young man who was teaching in a public school near the reservation; one-third of the students at this school were Native. He invited us to visit him and said he would try to introduce us to people who were "traditionalists;" those working to keep the traditions of the Mohawks and Iroquois alive.

This is how I met Ann Jock—the mother of several of

the students in his public school, and a clan mother in the tribe—and Tom Porter. The meeting with Tom Porter, which took place in a Long House, where Mohawks have met since before history was recorded on this continent, was a watershed moment for me because he introduced us to concepts I had never heard of before. He told us about the Iroquois Confederacy, which consisted of a number of tribes, of which the Mohawks were one. Other tribes had been invited to "take refuge under the Great Tree" if they were willing to follow the Great Law, which had been handed down to the Iroquois. The Great Law was a method by which people could live together in peace, not a racial concept but a spiritual one. He also explained the way in which the Iroquois made decisions, which has had a profound and lasting impact.

Over the next couple of years, we went back several times to participate in Social Dances—where we were invited to participate in traditional Native dances—and meet people, learn from them about their lives, and teach them about our school. In 1971, I got an urgent phone call from Ann Jock at one o'clock in the morning. She told me that 70 Mohawk children had been kicked out of the public high school because they wanted to learn their own language and culture. At that time, Mohawk students were actually punished if they spoke Mohawk in school because the teachers assumed that they were saying bad things about them behind their backs. Meanwhile, the language was dying; a whole generation of people no longer spoke their native tongue. Ann asked us if we could come to the reservation the next day, bring some of our students, bring slides, talk about our school and tell them how they could go about starting a school.

We made the two-hour trip the next day, giving a presentation in Ann's house, which was packed with parents and children. At one point we were asked whether they needed federal funds or state funds in order to start a school. We told them that they already had the resources they needed in their community; it wasn't necessary to find government funds. A week later Ann Jock and her children (she eventually had 15) and several others from the community started the Indian Way School in a small square building that they had constructed in their backyard. That building still stands and it has occurred to me that maybe it should be designated with a plaque and put on some national register; it was the beginning of the North American Indian Survival School Movement.

Over the next few years, and throughout the history of our school, we continued to have regular exchanges with the Mohawks at Akwesasne, the Native name for the area of Upstate New York, and with the Kahnewake, another Mohawk tribe just outside of Montreal. They would come and visit us at our school in Vermont, and we would bring groups of students from our school to visit them. A year after the first Indian Way School was started, a second one was started over the border in Kahnewake, known in Canada as Caughnawaga.

The school in New York never had any state funding and operated however they could on local funds. Ann dealt with some pushback from the traditionalist chiefs who felt she hadn't included them in the decision to start the school, and thus withheld their full support. However, the Indian Way School near Montreal had plenty of tribal support. After operating for a year or so, though, they decided to send a group to Ottawa and the Bureau of Indian Affairs to appeal for funding. While they weren't taken seriously at first, they eventually found a source of funding from the Quebec government that has continued to flow from that time on; the Indian Way School still exists more than 45 years later.

By this point René Lévesque, the Prime Minister of the Province of Quebec, had been elected. He was a proponent of Quebec separatism. He decided that all immigrants had to be educated in French in Quebec. He then decided that all Native Americans were immigrants. Well, even the non-traditionalist Mohawks knew they weren't immigrants and mounted a protest. They pulled their students out of the local schools, but since they had the Indian Way School as a model, instead of just keeping them out of school, they set up mini schools of about 15 students each across the reservation, led by Indian Way School staff.

After doing this for about a week, the parents were so surprised to see the positive changes in their children that they announced that this was no longer a protest, this was permanent, and that they were setting up the Survival School. The Canadian government, always happy to do anything that would oppose René Lévesque, said that they would pay for it. They eventually built a two-million-dollar facility along the St. Lawrence River, along with rope courses, a gymnasium, and a cafeteria, taking perhaps a third of the students out of the public schools.

Subsequently, the public school system agreed to

create a total immersion Mohawk language elementary school option. They hired Indian Way School staff, particularly Rita Phillips, who had been a teacher there for a long time, to write the appropriate curriculum. This option continues to this day.

Sometimes people wonder what the use is of setting up a small alternative school and keeping it going. In fact, the Indian Way School still continues, along with the Survival School and the public immersion Mohawk schools. This story shows that a small alternative model can lead to a change in the whole community. In this case, it helped preserve the Mohawk language and culture.

Chapter Six
Learning to Learn

Freedom for children is important but democracy is the key. Democratic schools can even have compulsory classes—if a meeting makes the ironic decision that they want to. I know of one school that, through their meeting, decided to have a compulsory class; it was called the Must Do Class. It happened two or three times week, the students and staff would gather for a 45 minute period in which someone would make a presentation, usually on a subject they thought was new to the group at large. Every year they would bring up the question of whether to have the Must Do Class and at any point the meeting could have voted against having it, but people seemed to feel it was worthwhile.

I believe it's important to allow teachers and staff in learner-centered schools to teach whatever they want and not to force them to teach in any particular field—just as the students deserve freedom to choose, so do the adults. If they hold knowledge and passion in an area and students are interested, they can offer that. However, it's equally important for teachers to teach things they initially know nothing about, because one of the most important things to learn is how to find the answers to questions and how to find the resources you need. For children, sharing an experience with an adult who is actively learning can be very, very useful.

Some schools think it is important to have teachers available and waiting for children to ask them for classes, rather than offering any set lessons. To me this sometimes seems as if the teachers are saying "Well, we have the answers but we're not going to tell you unless you ask us!" I think the students should be able to feel that staff members are open and will share anything that interests or excites them personally.

Along those same lines, what is the responsibility of a school to its students, in terms of creating an environment or giving them specific information about things that are possible, that they may not have known about and wouldn't discover unless someone took the time and almost forced them to learn? What happens if you are a teacher and you see a certain pattern in a student and you think it would be useful to them to point out that pattern?

It's not a simple thing and that's why teaching, especially in a democratic school, is more of an art than a science. You have to know when, based on the relationship you've built with a student, they would want to know certain information or get particular feedback and when it would be intrusive or stifling. While these waters take practice in navigating, I firmly believe that adults, as individuals and mentors of children, shouldn't be reluctant to share information that they think could be of interest to their students. A student should always have the ability to give feedback to the adult on whether or not their advice was worthwhile, and these exchanges continue to build relationship, trust, and care.

The role of adults in democratic schools are full of nuance. There are many questions that can arise about what adults should and should not do. For example, to what extent does that staff prepare the environment? Should school meetings get to approve every change in the physical plan or in the building? Should students be able to vote on hiring and firing? On a school's budget? Each school must figure the answers out for themselves. I do believe, though, that if you hire staff members in a school, you should trust them to do the work that you've hired them to do.

Many schools use the painful fact that the older children know they will soon be entering the "real world" to get them in line academically. Unless this focus on academics is coming from the students themselves, I think it is a mistake to do this. When Herb Snitzer of Lewis-Wadhams School was asked whether their children were prepared to enter public schools after their experience at Lewis-Wadhams, he said the best training for a bad experience is a good one. I couldn't agree more; if children have been in a situation in which they are confident in themselves as people and as learners, they can deal with anything.

It is clear that specific factual information is not very important in an age when people can quickly get whatever information they need. How much you've memorized doesn't matter so much anymore. The kind of testing emphasized by the mandated high-stakes tests and the whole accountability movement is not only not important, but counterproductive.

On the other hand, knowing how to find information

when you need it *is* important, and, if necessary, could be tested for. Instead of knowing if children have memorized a fact, maybe they could be tested on how quickly they could find an answer to something they don't know.

It may also be possible to structure tests for real accountability in education, tests for things like responsibility, interpersonal sensitivity, humanitarianism, creativity. With a fair amount of thought these things that we really value in alternative education could be measured, and the public schools could be measured for them, too. But beyond that there are additional questions, such as, why the preoccupation with measurement? And does this practice, if not asked for, violate students' human rights?

The Deweyan concept of reflection, of having to evaluate or review what experiences you have had, has been shown to be one of the ways you are able to reinforce what you learn. According to brain research, having regular sessions in which a person reflects on and evaluates their time spent—whether they've been participating in a class, playing with friends, or reading on their own— puts the learning they've done from short-term into long-term memory. Not only is this more effective than measurement-based testing, but it allows for students to once again be active participants in their learning process.

Many adults worry that children who are not forced to learn will become lazy. Personally, I don't believe in the idea of laziness. I think that human beings have a tendency to do the things they like to do and are interested in doing. If children grow up in a situation where they can continually choose the things they're interested in doing, they will not be seen as lazy. Not only that, but when these children get into various situations later, they will be better able to find things that they are interested in doing because they will be connected to that impulse in themselves. If you force children to study things that they are not interested in, that disinterest can come across as laziness, but also have the lasting effect of disconnecting children with what they enjoy doing when they are not being directed.

This feeling of connectedness has, in my experience, had lasting effect into students' adult professions. Many who went to mainstream schools, where their personal interests were not considered, expect their jobs to be the same: boring and uninteresting. On the other hand, I have consistently found that students who went to learner-centered schools, or who were homeschooled or unschooled, have gone into fields and jobs that interest them and enjoy their work.

It is true that some children are more self-motivated than others. Often, this is the result of the experiences they've had; what kind of school situation they've been in, what kind of parenting they've grown up with, what their learning environment was like. What I've also come to know is that it is impossible for anyone to tell just how much another person is learning. I've seen children who were supposedly lazy become very self-motivated when they got into a situation in which they could really pursue the things they were interested in. I've also been around students who appeared to be "doing nothing" when they were really taking in their surroundings and learning a lot.

For instance, I once had a student when he was very young, at about five years old, and then later, after having lived out of state, he returned to Shaker Mountain at the age of twelve. Through the first few months of that year it didn't seem he was doing much of anything in the school and in the meetings. He was present, but he would close his eyes and go to sleep. Whenever he was called on, however, he would immediately say, "I'm not sleeping, I'm just resting." That caused us to make a rule that "You can't *appear* to be sleeping in the meeting!"

After a period of time there was a general agreement that he should go to a different school the next year because he didn't seem to be getting much out of ours. To help facilitate his transition, we gave him a basic test and according to the results, he had gone up an average of three grade levels. He had been in fifth grade and would be going into sixth grade but we recommended seventh grade on the basis of the tests. He did so well once he started in his public school that they put him in eighth grade.

How this happened is still somewhat of a mystery, but it proves the point that each person's process is different, and that each person's journey in education looks unique. How foolish, then, to require that we all adhere to a standard that will accurately represent so few of us! Another person's learning is something that we may support and encourage, but it's not something we can control. Freedom is the key to unleashing this power that all children to have.

Chapter Seven
Adults and Freedom at School

How powerful should adults in a democratic community be? The answer depends on the individual community. Ideally, adults can just be themselves and say what's on their mind and if they're strong people, there will be other strong people in the community who can react and, when necessary, stand up to them and disagree with confidence. The freedom of all people to be themselves, to express their ideas and opinions unequivocally gives the community a better chance to come up with good decisions than if some individuals hold themselves back for fear of being too powerful.

That being said, sometimes students need time to become comfortable openly disagreeing with adults—especially if they've never been allowed or encouraged to do so! If meetings are consistently dominated with adult voices, it may be worth taking notice and stepping back. A good way to get more students involved is to ask them questions: What do you think would be a good solution? What would be a fair compromise? If you were in charge, what would you decide?

Even at democratic schools, there are times when

adults need to make firm decisions, without the input of the entire community, particularly when it comes to health and safety. There are countless instances of parents or teachers who haven't gone through the process of learning about freedom for themselves, and as a result, they've tended to overreact in the opposite direction; they are too hesitant to give their opinion or put their foot down in a situation when they see that something bad may be about to happen. And then sometimes something terrible does happen.

In moments when an adult must be the final voice, transparency can be a great tool. Be open about why you are making the decision, invite questions, discuss your reasoning. For instance, "Playing dodgeball around these chemistry sets is dangerous because glass could break and people could get hurt. We can either stop playing dodgeball in this room, or find another place for the chemistry sets." This sort of discussion is inclusive and raises the students' awareness of their surroundings as well; it also eliminates any suspicion that adults may be acting arbitrarily.

Democratic schools are good for adults, too, but it's a challenging job. For adults who have don't have direct experience in a democratic school, the learning curve can be steep. It's best if new hires have at least a theoretical understanding, but something harder to screen for are the inherent instincts to listen to and respect children. While the best training is to actually do it, it's wise to have supportive staff meetings, a designated mentor, or resources available so that the adults can continue to educate themselves on the philosophy. Sometimes, even with a lot of support, some adults don't work out and it's best that they no longer participate.

It's also important for the adults in a democratic school to be able to hold a balance. The needs of everybody in the school community must be met, adults as well as students. Getting too far away from that can create burnout. Burnout can happen when the needs of the individual adults in the community are not being met as they focus entirely on the needs of the students. It can also happen when adults don't take the time to evaluate how they're feeling, what challenges they're facing, and what they need. As I said, many adults in democratic schools are not the products of a democratic or alternative school; they may not be good enough at sticking up for themselves and demanding that their own needs be met. It is a potential problem people have to work through, to either learn about and grow from, or unfortunately in some cases, get burned out and leave.

Adults in a community need to understand that a lot of their instincts will be counter to what they're experiencing because of their own history in school. Even though I have seen amazing things happen with students in alternative and democratic schools over and over again, they continually surprise me because in my own education I was a product of a traditional system in which these miracles didn't happen.

Sometimes when you follow your gut, your gut tells you a child shouldn't have freedom and it won't work. But on the other hand, if you suppress the things that you feel, you can risk not being genuine, and the students may miss out on some of the ideas that you have that they might benefit from or really value. All you can do is use your best judgment and be open with the students about your own learning. Again, the more experience that you have with a real functioning democratic community, the more likely you are to make good decisions.

Democratic process has to evolve over a period of time so that the students and staff come to realize that they must deal with issues as they present themselves and as a team. They can't sweep difficult issues under the rug, otherwise these things will come back to haunt them. It's also helpful not to go into a meeting with a set idea about how an issue should be resolved. The end result is always going to be a creative combination of ideas, and remaining interested in what others think, trusting that the students have insight into the problem—instead of assuming that you alone know how to solve it—will foster the best outcome.

Staff members at democratic schools have another group, aside from the students, to care for: the parents. In many schools, teachers and directors are beginning to realize they can be more effective with the students if the parents are more familiar with the philosophy of the school and understand it on a deeper level.

There are different ways to encourage this familiarity. For example, the Grassroots Free School in Florida, required that any prospective parent read the book *Summerhill*. Other schools have workshops, parent support groups, or spend time during parent-teacher conferences focusing on philosophy. While parents shouldn't be unduly influential in the daily life of the school, parents who are supportive of the school and understand its basic philosophy are more apt to allow their children the freedom they need to flourish.

Freedom is much more complex than people realize. It's a process and a dynamic, rather than something that is tangible. That's what makes it so tricky and what makes the word so difficult to define. Any individual freedom will mean different things in different situations. Am I free to live anywhere I want right now? Technically, I am, but practically, I'm not. There's nothing that's stopping me from going anyplace I want, but I may be inhibited by money, transportation, available homes. Does this mean I don't have the freedom to move or does it mean that I've chosen to stay? Well, you could say I accept the circumstances I'm in and that's the decision that I've made.

With freedom in schools the same is true: each child must look at the circumstance that he or she is in. For example, you could tell students in a given alternative school that they are free to use the Internet all day long if they want, but if you only have one computer, their freedom is restricted—they don't individually have the freedom to use the Internet as much as they want.

Adults in democratic schools must be constant companions to the students as they navigate what their freedom means, how it relates to others, and how it influences the choices they make. It's subtle and complex and its exploration leads to tremendous growth and learning.

Chapter Eight
My Early Journey

In 1968, I started Shaker Mountain. In the years prior, I'd worked in various settings with children as I formulated thoughts and ideas on education. I began my journey as an undergraduate at Goddard College, and after an inspiring visit, worked for a year at Lewis-Wadhams School, which was founded by Herb Snitzer and modeled very closely to Summerhill. Later, after earning my Master's Degree at Antioch, I worked for a while at Elm Hill, the first group home for state foster children in Vermont, and helped it get off the ground.

I wondered, though, if it were possible to do something with a similar philosophy to Summerhill in a public school, so I got a job working with remedial reading students and underachievers at a public high school. I worked there for a year and had very good results with the children, running the program like a democratic school within the school. Because I ran the program during their free periods, every student was in there by choice. I wrote a little diary about it called, "I Was a Spy in the Public Schools." Over time, however, I realized that in a public school it was more likely that the system would change you than that you would change the system.

Shaker Mountain started small. At first we met in different spaces and traveled around in our car. We had a Plymouth and, before getting the storefront building on Pitkin Street, almost decided to call the school the Plymouth School. We had no boarding students until the third year, but we did have staff who lived at what would become the boarding part of the school, out at my place in Starksboro. That's about all we could provide because we didn't have much money.

There were good years and bad years at Shaker Mountain and it partly depended upon the quality of student leadership at the time. Over the years we found an approach that really worked well. Our decision-making process evolved over time, but the concept we pioneered—inspired by the Iroquois—held us in good stead. It is certainly the thing that we spent most of our time on and really specialized in. The value of the meeting goes right to the empowerment of each student—and each staff member, for that matter—and to the respect for each individual and their rights as a member of the school community.

We had meetings on Monday and Friday morning, each of which would have many items on the agenda, and was where all of the decisions that ran the school were made. If something came up between meetings, a person could call an emergency meeting at any time by ringing a meeting bell, which was an old fire bell. In contrast to other schools, where a person needed permission, we empowered students to ring the bell when they felt necessary, no matter others' opinions.

The school rule was that if there were classes going on, people did not have to leave the classes to go to a meeting. Whoever went to the meeting, however, would make the decision for the school. Permanent decisions couldn't be made unless they were at one of the regularly scheduled Monday or Friday meetings, and decisions that were made in the interim were reviewable by the regular meeting.

At the start of our meetings whoever wanted to be chairperson would say so. The whole process took place very quickly. One of the reasons for that was that we had lots of meetings and there wasn't great prestige in running a meeting. It was hard work. People were aware of that, but they also wanted to elect a good chairperson so the meeting would go smoothly. So several people would usually say they wanted to be chairperson, there would be an immediate vote, and whoever got the most votes would simply start chairing the meeting.

If that person got tired at some point, they could give the chairpersonship to somebody else. Or if somebody thought the chairperson wasn't running the meeting well, or that his or her attention was lagging, anybody could call for a new chairperson at which point there was a vote immediately, up or down. If the majority did not vote for selecting a new chairperson, the chairperson simply continued.

The chairperson would go through the agenda while the log-taker kept track of all the items on the agenda. The chairperson's job was to keep people on task, on the subject, keep everything moving smoothly, call on people in order and bring businesses to the vote. If you had a specific question to ask somebody during a business meeting, the person could answer that question—they didn't have to wait to be called on.

Sometimes the chairperson would ask another person

to keep track of the hands to make sure she got the order right. Generally she would follow that order unless there was some important reason not to. For example, if the meeting was about a particular person, she might let that person respond more often.

*****

Shaker Mountain had no set curriculum and very few classes that were regularly scheduled. Instead, each morning there were class announcements, and any activity whatsoever was called a class: playing racquetball was a class, organizing a trip to the Bahamas was a class. Eventually we had three vans available all the time, so we were constantly going all around the city to different places or activities, and these trips, too, were called classes.

At the end of the week we had evaluations in which we made a list of the things we had done and each student picked a staff member who would go over any individual problems or questions and help them think about and complete their evaluations. This reflection helped draw more from what could seem like frivolous activities; maybe it was during racquetball, for example, that a student overcame an obstacle, a fear, a conflict with a friend.

At the end of the year, we made a list of all the different activities, usually around 350, and the children would check off all of the things they participated in. We used this information to create transcripts, written by staff or, on occasion, the students themselves.

I was always surprised at how lucky we were to get

good teachers, even though we paid far less than any other local school. Over a period of time I came to realize several things. One is that it wasn't just luck. Because we paid so little, we almost never hired a teacher who was there for the money. They joined our staff because they believed in what we were doing; they wanted to empower students. We also had a system in which teachers received intensive feedback, in and out of our two weekly staff meetings. Often the new teachers weren't very good, but they were soon getting instant feedback because no students would go to their classes. They either adapted or left.

Many teachers in the public school system never learn that lesson because they have a captive audience. Non-compulsory class attendance, though, creates a situation in which the content must be valued, relevant, and presented dynamically; the ability to come up with such a class, or work with students to create such a course, is key in the training and development of alternative school teachers.

Obviously, though, teaching of classes wasn't the only thing teachers needed to be able to do; they had to be able to get along with individual children, as well as other staff members. They also needed to be getting something out of the experience themselves; personal growth among adults is just as important as it is among students.

At Shaker Mountain we had something called the Stop Rule. The Stop Rule was based on the idea that, for a lot of children, conflict arises because they haven't clearly communicated to the other person. For example, sometimes children would be wrestling and they'd be having fun. Then all of a sudden one of the children didn't want to wrestle anymore, but the other child didn't realize it. The child could say, "Stop," and in one word communicate all of the possibilities: I don't want to do this anymore, I'm being annoyed by it, I feel like I really want to fight about it, whatever. The Stop Rule had the power to halt the situation from escalating so that conversation could take place, personal boundaries could be set and respected, and conflict resolved.

In meetings about conflict, a key question was always, "Did you use the Stop Rule?" If a person hadn't stopped, thus breaking the Stop Rule, it was a serious transgression. The community also understood that the Stop Rule could be abused, and set to creating rules to prohibit this. For instance, you couldn't say to someone, "Stop breathing so loud; it's annoying me." That would be unreasonable. You also couldn't antagonize someone and then hide behind the Stop Rule; like poke someone then say "stop" as a way to inhibit their reaction. The Stop Rule had power because the students and staff gave it power; it is a prime example of an agreement that works to uphold the health and integrity of that community. Instead of being handed down by an arbitrary adult authority, the implementation and accountability was held largely by the students, who regularly discussed and tweaked rules to better meet their needs.

*****

For a prospective student, Shaker Mountain had a long trial period and an admissions committee that decided who was accepted. There was a Visiting Week, after which—if the admissions committee thought it had been successful—there was a Trial Week.

The admissions committee could choose to extend either the Visiting or Trial Week. Usually, these were extended if a person was having trouble demonstrating the responsibility needed to be part of the community. Sometimes, coming from another school situation, this meant they needed more time to adjust, but ultimately, if they weren't able to show in a few weeks that they could handle it, it was usually not in our best interest—or theirs—to take them on as a student.

It is exceptionally hard for many schools to break ties with a student when the relationship—for whatever reason—isn't working. Often communities, because of their best intentions, will overextend themselves to work with a student or family; in these cases, the final breaking point can be more painful than it needs to be, because it has been dragged out for so long. It is important to have mechanisms in place to deal with these kinds of situations, because in every school, they will happen. This is also why a long admissions process can be a boon to a school community; it gives everyone a chance to get to know each other up front, without having to make a firm commitment.

At Shaker Mountain, if a student who had already been through the admissions process was struggling, the meeting had the power to actually send children back to the admissions committee for another trial period. This served as a kind of last chance; a way for the community to make its needs clear and an opportunity for the student to work to develop the controls needed to come back as full members of the community.

It didn't happen often that a student was asked to leave the school, but during the 17 years that I ran Shaker Mountain, I noticed an odd thing happening. In the instances in which someone had been asked to leave the school, many of them returned five or six years later, either wanting to be a staff member or touch base to tell us what had happened after they left. It was very rare that any anger or bitterness towards the school existed. The process by which those decisions were made, the painstaking care and patience involved, worked to set a standard that— even if the initial parting was painful—had a long lasting effect. Maybe at the heart of all this is the idea that once you get brought into a community, even if eventually the community has to reject you, in some way you will always be part of the community. You become part of the fabric.

Many of the students at Shaker Mountain, particularly with the boarding students, were children who'd had very difficult life experiences before they came to us. They'd been abandoned, abused, and so on. This is something you see in many alternative schools, not just democratic schools.

Remarkably, though, the environment we created at our school allowed them to live their subsequent lives as if they had been in a privileged, nurturing home. While their backgrounds may lead outsiders to believe that they were destined for self-destruction, depression, or violence, they have lived full, whole lives; aware of who they are, how they learn, and what they love. While we didn't necessarily think of ourselves as an intentional community, it became

clear that, because we operated as a family, each person—
adult or child—who spent time with us, was thankful they
had been a part of the community.

Chapter Nine

Connections Beyond School

P eople worry that alternative schools can be isolated communities. I do get concerned about schools which, for example, are not doing a lot of field trips, not going out into their communities a lot, and are pretty much staying in their building. In the end, of course, the children are still going to be able to cope with whatever situation they have to deal with, if the basic process is good. But it is better if you have a school that is interfacing a lot with its community.

This is what we did at Shaker Mountain. We were right in the downtown of our city, so people couldn't really ask the question, "What happens when you're in the real world?" We were in the real world all the time. Students were continuously going off to do internships or visiting the library or exploring other places in the area and using them as resources. Probably half the school was off in the community every day. Our three vehicles were constantly being used to facilitate activities and adventures.

For example, one day a student named Danny asked what he would need to do to get a pilot's license. So we went yelling around the school for anyone who was interested in "Danny's Pilot License Class" to get into the van. Then we tried to figure out where we ought to go. We decided to go to the local airport and ask them what someone would need to do to get a pilot's license.

An airport employee directed us next door, where we talked to the manager of their flight-training program. He explained to us what someone would need to learn and told us that trainees had to fly so many solo hours. Then one of the pilots came in and the manager said to him, "Why don't you show them the cockpit?"

As the pilot showed us the small plane he'd just been flying in, the manager yelled out the door, "Why don't you take them for a spin?" So we wound up flying over our school—all of this within an hour of the time that Danny asked how he could get a pilot's license! This is the kind of thing that you would not have happening in an ordinary school. Anything was possible. The sky was not a limit!

There are many differences between the world then and now, including things like liability which can prevent such great adventures from taking place spur of the moment. It's important for schools to remember, though, that there are still great resources available in any community and with planning, students can participate in the real world right now. It's one of the many great benefits of alternative schools; not being beholden to a classroom and desks leaves the world wide open.

*****

At Shaker Mountain, when we traveled in small groups we had trip meetings. One thing that differed from our regular school meetings was that when we were on a trip it was understood that whoever organized the trip, usually a staff member, had the power to make decisions for the group, especially in urgent situations. We couldn't be stopping every five minutes to have a meeting to decide things.

This made the working dynamic a little different and it would have to be formally acknowledged by the people who signed up to go on the trip. The kinds of things that usually were decided democratically had to do with what things we wanted to do and where we wanted to go, but also interpersonal things. It's amazing how changing locations can bring up all sorts of things!

We did a lot of traveling beyond our immediate area, too; our vans took us to almost every place you could go in North America; Florida, California, Mexico City, British Columbia, Vancouver, New Brunswick, Prince Edward Island, and Nova Scotia.

One year, though, a student brought up in a meeting that they would like to have us go on a school trip off the continental United States. We batted this around for a while, a trip group was announced, and in the trip group we discussed some of the closest places we could get to outside of the USA. We looked at a map and realized that one of the closest countries off the continent was the Bahamas.

Of course at that point, and throughout the history of the school, we had no budget for travel. If we'd had a small budget, we would probably have been limited as to where we could go on school trips. However, since we had no budget whatsoever, we could go anyplace we wanted to!

There was no limit because it was incumbent upon

each trip group to come up with their own funding, and the students at Shaker Mountain developed many different ways of funding their trips. Sometimes they would do things in advance, like having an auction or a special event of some sort. Sometimes they would get local sponsors. For this they would have a sponsor sheet, which would say, "I'm a student at Shaker Mountain School and I have a chance to go on a trip and would you be interested in getting involved in the process of sponsoring me?" We would sometimes raise quite a bit of money in a short period of time.

In this case we made a phone call to an 800 number for the Bahamas Tourist Bureau and asked them whether, if we came to the Bahamas, they would be able to find a place to put our sleeping bags down and places where we could speak about alternative education. They got back to us and said that the People to People Organization would be very interested in having us come, that they had places for us to speak, schools that were interested in having us visit, and that the Orange Hill Guest House had agreed to let us stay there, with our sleeping bags.

We called the airlines and said that the people of the Bahamas had invited us to come there, that they have places for us to sleep, places for us to speak, and schools to visit—all we needed was transportation. So you can see that we put this together like a puzzle. The first couple of airlines turned us down but the third one we called, Bahamas Air, said they might be interested in helping us but that they only flew from Miami. Of course our school was in Vermont, 1,500 miles away.

We had a trip meeting and made a decision about

what to do. We voted to go for it. We decided to work our way down to Florida and hope that perhaps Bahamas Air would be able to make some kind of arrangement for us.

We worked our way down the East coast, speaking at colleges, passing the hat, stopping at restaurants and cleaning parking lots in exchange for meals. Finally we made our way to Florida.

At one point, on the way down, we called the airline's public relations person and told him we were on the way to Florida. He now said he would be able to give us the tickets at half price. We told him to forget it. We couldn't afford that. These were low-income students. He told us to keep in touch.

We actually went past Miami into the Keys. We found a motel that had some rooms that they weren't going to be able to clean till the morning and the children talked them into letting us put our sleeping bags down there. The students got good at doing those things. I think if you can do that, you can talk to anybody in life about anything.

Then we called the public relations person at the airline again and he said that he would donate tickets to all of the children but we had to get to the airport in Miami the next day. So we drove up to Miami and got on the plane. They flew us to the Bahamas.

We were met by the Lutheran church bus which took us to the Orange Hill Guest House, right on the ocean. Then they started taking us around the island to the various schools that we wanted to visit. They even had a banquet at one of them in our honor.

It was a great trip but in some ways quite a shocking experience for our students, and an interesting one, because they came from a state that was 99 percent white and they were now in a country that seemed to be almost the same percentage black. I remember a student at one of the schools in the Bahamas asking our students, "What do you do if they call you a honky?" And the Vermonters looked at each other blankly. We were there for five days, then we flew back to Miami and we worked our way back up to Vermont.

Chapter Ten
Alternative School History

The alternative education movement goes back well before there was a name for it. In fact, what we now call alternative education and homeschooling was the norm for humankind for millennia. It could be argued that the current public school system is just a relatively short experiment, spanning only 150 years or so.

Horace Mann is often called "the father of American Public Education." Through his efforts the underpinnings of the current public school system were created, starting in the 1840s. Although his intentions were noble—to help masses of "illiterate" and "uneducated" children—he was strongly influenced by a visit to study the education system in Prussia, which was very authoritarian.

The newly created public school system was revolutionary and well intentioned, but from the very beginning it was following the first paradigm. For example, Mann said that one of its purposes was to create obedient and compliant citizens. The public school system also fits very nicely with an industrial model: students are fed the same facts at the same time, and they are moved through the system at intervals, from one grade to another, with the same expectation.

Education critic John Gatto, in his book *Weapons of Mass Instruction*, cited this quote by H.L. Mencken in 1924:

> The aim of public education is NOT "...to fill the young of the species with knowledge and awaken their intelligence...Nothing could be further from the truth. The aim . . . is simply to reduce as many individuals as possible to the same safe level, to breed and train a standardized citizenry, to put down dissent and originality. That is its aim in the United States...and that it is its aim everywhere else."

In contrast, the ideas behind a learner-centered approach have popped up throughout history, perhaps because they work. One early proponent was Jean Jacques Rousseau, whose *Emile*, also known as *On Education*, was based on these ideas. *Emile* was banned in Paris and Geneva and was publicly burned in 1762, the year of its first publication. Ironically, during the French Revolution, it served as the inspiration for what became a new national system of education.

In North America, Bronson Alcott, who was largely self-educated, founded a series of controversial schools in the 1830s in the Philadelphia and Boston area. He was influenced by European reformers such as Johann Heinrich Pestalozzi and Friedrich Froebel.

His Temple School was a forerunner of progressive and democratic schooling. It caused a lot of controversy because he accepted an African American girl and refused to expel her. Many parents withdrew their students and soon he was left with just a handful, including his own daughter Louisa May Alcott. She famously went on to write books such as *Little Men* and *Little Women*, based largely on her experiences in her father's alternative school. Many of Alcott's educational principles are still used in classrooms today, including "teach by encouragement," art education, music education, acting exercises, learning through experience, risk-taking in the classroom, tolerance in schools, physical education/recess, and early childhood education.

*****

Other pioneers in the learner-centered approach around the turn of the century include Francisco Ferrer, Maria Montessori, Rudolph Steiner, and John Dewey. Francisco Ferrer was an anarchist in Spain who founded the Modern School movement. His schools were democratic, coeducational, and not affiliated with religion, which was unprecedented at that time. At one point, there were as many as 200 Modern Schools in Spain and many others around the world, including one in New York City.

Maria Montessori was born and grew up in Italy. Graduating with a math-physics degree at age 20, she decided to pursue a degree in medicine, unheard of at the time for a woman. Despite opposition and hostility she became a doctor and started to practice medicine in 1897.

After working in a psychiatric clinic she began to work with mentally disabled children. She worked in a school for such children while teaching courses for university students and developing materials. The students in the school were considered "uneducable," yet later many passed tests for "normal" children.

In 1907 she began to apply her ideas to mainstream children, at first working with low income families in Rome. She refined her ideas, giving children freedom to pick materials that interested them, and coming and going to different spaces as they wished. Now there are thousands of Montessori Schools around the world and over 5,000 in the USA, including many which are publicly funded.

Rudolph Steiner was an Austrian philosopher, author, and spiritualist. He founded the religious society of Anthroposophy, which was an outgrowth of the field of Theosophy. This was partially a result of his work in trying to merge science and spirituality. He also did pioneering work in biodynamic agriculture, without the use of pesticides and chemical fertilizers.

He built the first Waldorf school in 1919, based on his ideas, in Stuttgart, Germany. Waldorf schools believe that dance, art, and music are as important as other academics. His ideas about democracy and social reform earned him the wrath of Adolph Hitler, who said that his Anthroposophy was incompatible with National Socialist racial ideology. Although he died just a few years later, there are now thousands of Waldorf schools around the world, more that 100 in the USA, including public Waldorf models, and many more Waldorf-inspired schools.

A commonality shared by all the people who have

approached this important reality of alternative education is that children are natural learners. The original definition of the word "education" related to the concept of educating or drawing out of people the learning that is inherent in them. The public school system has the opposite assumption. It treats children as empty vessels that need to be filled up with facts or information, rather than as people who already have a natural curiosity and interest in learning.

Similarly, John Dewey's work goes back to before the beginning of the 20th century. Many schools, generally known as "progressive schools" were inspired by his ideas; he is often credited with the creation of the idea of progressive education. Born in Burlington, Vermont, Dewey's basic idea was that children learn best from direct experience, from taking some responsibility, and from working directly with their hands. One of the many schools inspired by Dewey and the progressive movement is called City and Country, located in New York City. It began before the First World War and continues to this day.

Dewey eventually wound up teaching at Columbia University Teachers College in New York City, and wrote a book called *Democracy in Education*. Contrary to the concept of democracy within schools that we've been discussing, Dewey was more focused on preparing students for democracy when they grew up than practicing it within schools.

As more and more progressive schools emerged, more of the graduates began to apply to colleges and universities. In contrast to public schools, however, students from progressive schools didn't come with any grade history. As a result, the Progressive Education Association conducted the Eight Year Study, from 1932-1940. The goal was to try to evaluate the progressive system and the students participating. The Eight-Year Study (also known as the Thirty-School Study) stands today as one of the most definitive studies of a learner-centered approach, as opposed to a curriculum-driven one. Students from the most experimental, nonstandard schools earned markedly higher academic achievement rates than those in traditional schools, and even other progressive schools. The results of the study showed that students from progressive schools also did better in college, and after college, than the students from the traditional schools.

*****

In the early 1960s the free school movement was jump-started with the publication of the book *Summerhill*; thousands of free schools were created within the next fifteen years. Summerhill was the first specifically democratic school, established in 1921 by A.S. Neill. Neill was a Scottish teacher who didn't want to replicate the kind of education that he'd grown up with. In England, he became a famous radical writer on education before he had any thought of starting a school. In 2015, they celebrated the 100th anniversary of Neill's publication of *A Dominie's Log*, about his experiences as a new teacher.

In the creation of Summerhill, Neill was very much influenced by Homer Lane, an American who went to

England to start a therapeutic community for troubled youth, called The Little Commonwealth. Lane had already created similar democratic programs, within reformatories for boys, in the United States.

Neill was 38 when he started Summerhill and he ran it for 52 years until he died at age 90.

In the wake of the publication of *Summerhill,* there was an explosion in the creation of free schools that continued for over a decade. The average life of a new free school was about 18 months. But some of them are still around, such as Clonlara, in Michigan and Sudbury Valley School in Massachusetts (both founded in 1967). Also, The Grassroots Free School in Tallahassee, Florida, and The Free School in Albany, New York.

Currently, Summerhill has from 75 to 90 students ranging in age from 5 to 18, although most students leave at 16 to go to "college," which is the way the English system works. They have about a dozen staff members, house parents, and teachers who instruct in specific areas. There is a timetable of classes that students can choose to go to or not. Up to 20 of the students are day students and the rest are boarding. Some of the younger children tend to be day school students whose parents have moved to the area.

Summerhill also has a cleaning staff and a cooking staff, although some of the students and teachers are also involved in the cooking and serving process. The meals are delivered regularly at set times.

I think there has always been a belief at Summerhill that you need to have a stable situation of sleeping arrangements, sleeping times, eating times and so on, which will help establish a secure routine for the children. They will then have a certain basis for their existence that they can count on. I remember that was also the case at Lewis-Wadhams.

Most things are subject to the school meeting and over time, Summerhill has changed the way it manages its meetings. In 2002, when it grew from about 60 or 70 students to 90 they shifted from having a tribunal to deal with students who broke the school laws to having a short meeting three times a week. Everything goes through that meeting and anything can be put on the agenda.

Like all democratic schools, though, they've decided where limitations exist. For instance, changes in bedtimes can be decided at a meeting, but I don't think they could fire all the cooking staff and take over the cooking themselves. There are certain areas over which the director retains power; the hiring and firing of staff, and whether a student needs to leave the school.

It was interesting to see that a long-established school like Summerhill was able to change the way they did something so central to the life of the school. It shows, though, that schools need to remain adaptable to time and the community—if a system that has worked for many years suddenly doesn't fit well with the population, it is in everyone's best interest if it is changed.

Another interesting detail about Summerhill is that it is a proprietary school, unlike many democratic schools which are non-profit. As such, when Neill passed away, ownership and directorship passed to his wife, Ena.

Likewise, when she passed in 1997, their daughter, Zoë became the owner and director.

Many schools use a non-profit board in which case there is actually a legal body, whether an individual owner or a group like a board of trustees, which technically controls the school. Soon after Zoë took over as principal, the school hit a crucial time in the 90s when Summerhill came under attack from the educational establishment in England. A decision had to be made about how to approach this crisis. Many people were encouraging her to compromise with the government and to capitulate to their demands.

What Zoë eventually decided was, "Yes, we can fix the walls, we can fix the toilets, but when it comes to the philosophy of the school and non-compulsory classes, we are not willing to change and we will fight that right up to the top court in England, and if we fail in that, then we will close the school. We will never have a Summerhill School that has compulsory classes."

Summerhill won the fight in 1999 and since that time Zoë and Summerhill seem to be thriving. Recently, when the government education department started to renege on decisions that were made in the court case, Summerhill decided to remove itself from the jurisdiction of the state school system and come under the auspices of the English independent school association and its inspections.

Zoë has said she believes that if Summerhill were not proprietary and was run by a board, it would have given in to the government and abandoned its philosophy years ago. It is an interesting question. For those schools that operate with a board, it provides an impetus to make sure that board is made up of people who really believe in the philosophy of the school and who are willing to fight for it in the face of great obstacles.

*****

The whole idea of democratic process is one that always seemed obvious and natural to me. When I started my first recreation center, while I was at Goddard College in 1962, it ran as a democracy. This was before I had ever read *Summerhill* or heard of it. When I started Shaker Mountain in 1967, I don't think that I was aware that there was any kind of large movement of free schools. This was probably true of many of the other thousands of people who started little schools. Only gradually did we realize that there was some kind of movement and try to coalesce and organize it in some way.

In the 1970s the alternative school movement expanded into public schools. The first ones were for any interested students and are now called "choice" public alternatives. School Within a School in Brookline, Massachusetts (1971), City as School in New York City, and Alternative Community School in Ithaca, New York (1974) are all examples which continue into the 21st century. The New Orleans Free School started as a private free school in the early 1970s but uniquely became a public magnet school and survived many attempts to close it down until it closed after Hurricane Katrina. Its history and struggle are documented in the book, *Flood of Conflict*.

In the late '70s and early '80s, under the guidance

of John Holt, parents around the United States began homeschooling their children in large numbers. Holt had been a long-term school critic and promoter of alternative schools. He eventually wrote *Teach Your Own,* and rejected the concept of school altogether.

There are now an estimated two million homeschoolers or more in the United States, and the movement has spread to other countries. For example, there are at least 100,000 now in England. It is legal in most countries but, surprisingly, illegal in countries such as Germany, Sweden, and the Netherlands.

In 1991, Joe Nathan's group started the first Charter School in Minnesota. Joe had visited us at Shaker Mountain several years earlier when he was studying Vermont's voucher system. This first charter launched the charter school movement, again inspired by a desire to make education more relevant and learner centered. There are now over 6,500 charter schools (as of 2013-14). Some people are concerned that the movement has been taken over by corporations. But the potential is still there to have learner-centered charter schools and there are several examples of them.

People continue to be dissatisfied with the traditional, standardized, top-down approach of the traditional system. The movement continues. Moving forward through the rest of the book we'll talk more about what has happened since the '90s and what is happening today.

Chapter Eleven
Public Alternatives

To have a full-scale democratic system you have to have the authority to truly empower people. Or you can do something like what John Gatto did in what he called his "guerrilla curriculum." That is, decide as a teacher that you need to become like a spy and go underground and try to give students a forum to make decisions, even though you know you're not allowed to do so. Some teachers have done this; sometimes it's worked and sometimes they've been fired.

I know that John Gatto used to try to sneak his students out of the classroom and into the community to do experiential projects and then cover for them. That's one way of doing it. But generally speaking, you need to have authority that you can actually give to students to make decisions. That's a first requirement. Beyond that you have to have educators who believe that students have the right to make these decisions and that the decisions will be better than if they were made arbitrarily by an administration. If you don't have that basic belief in your bones, then I don't know how you can do it.

There is an intrinsic problem with using democratic systems in public school classrooms. The system, being inherently authoritarian, gives a lot of arbitrary power to the administration. These schools tend to attract people who are authoritarian and who like to have that power, or who, at the very least, believe that the traditional model is the best way to educate. Those teachers don't want to empower students and listen to them; either because they don't believe children deserve those rights or they don't believe it's necessary.

A lot of the problems with public schools go back to the roots of the public education system. Well documented in John Gatto's books, the system was not really designed to democratize or to teach democracy or to get people ready to function in a democratic society. The roots of the system were more to do with certain political agendas when the system was created.

For example, a lot of Protestants in the United States, the majority at the time, were very much afraid of the influx of Catholics who were pouring into the country in the 1800s and so they wanted to Protestantize them. That was one of the motivations for the public school system.

Another was to get people ready to work in factories because we were in the middle of the industrial revolution. They wanted people to be prepared to follow orders, to change what they were doing at the sound of a bell. All of those things were not conducive to encouraging a democratic or open society. They came from a political agenda. What we have today is really the logical extension of a system that had those roots.

Of course, who is to say this isn't still the political agenda of some people in power? Naturally it's easier for the people in charge if they are not being questioned or challenged. It makes it easier for them to do the things they want to do.

We don't have many political leaders who really want to empower people democratically, and who want to come up with creative ideas and get the input of constituents. Maybe that's because they are all people who came out of our undemocratic educational system. In fact, this could be another reason why we don't have lots of democratic schools. It is certainly one of the reasons why it is such an uphill fight to create them. It may be one reason why some people seem to crave authoritarian political leaders, in the USA and in Russia since the coup.

In most schools no significant decisions are made by the students. This is partly because the people in charge don't want students to recognize that they might have the right to make significant decisions. Also, it would just make things more complicated and more difficult for the administrators. The simplest thing, of course, is to have an authoritarian system in which the people in the administration make all the decisions. What they may not realize is that they could go a long way toward solving their bullying problem if they supported a more democratic system.

Public schools could begin to have some effective democracy, even if the decisions were limited to specific areas. But to make the transition in a public school system is difficult because the public school system is set up everywhere as an authoritarian system, with various levels of power and decision-making authority. I don't know of a single school district anywhere in the United States in which all major decisions are made democratically and involve students. There are individual programs and individual schools but I don't know of any place where there's a whole district.

Real change has to happen on at least a district level. Otherwise what will need to happen, and what does seem to be happening, is for millions of people simply to go around the system. They will have to opt out. This is now more hopeful than anything happening within the system.

I don't believe that there is any easy answer to it. At one point I thought that what was happening in District 4 in New York City was going to be precedent setting.

At that time Debbie Meier came to this district when it was the lowest scoring district of the 32 districts in New York City on almost any standardized tests. It was in Spanish Harlem. The superintendent gave Debbie a school to do what she wanted with, to see if she could do something different. She then set up the Central Park East Alternative School.

This was a school in which the students could learn in a relaxed environment. The teachers were empowered to make a lot of decisions about how they wanted to teach. The students could wander around the building and they could work on the floor, for example. It was so effective that they immediately set up Central Park East 2 and started a process by which they eventually created a lot of alternative schools within this district. Then they took some big schools and waited until they failed, or almost failed, and broke them up into smaller schools within their old buildings.

Eventually they had 55 schools in 20 buildings. It seemed very exciting. The average reading score in that district went from the bottom to the middle and they even began to have more white children coming into the district, than leaving it, every day. In Spanish Harlem!

Unfortunately these ideas didn't spread to other districts. I once thought that when they demonstrated the effectiveness of these ideas, other districts in New York City would start moving in the same direction. But that didn't happen. There were only a few other alternative schools established around New York City.

It seems to be that Debbie Meier's model empowered teachers but it didn't empower students. I remember having a discussion with Debbie about this and she said she didn't want to have a democratic decision-making process or have meetings in these schools that would end up being phony. So, rather than have one that was phony, like a student council, she wasn't going to have anything and she never did.

Her focus was on teacher empowerment, which was in itself a problem in the city. That is the basis on which the alternative schools that exist in New York City have been established and therefore to my knowledge there is not actually any democratic school in New York City. When we were both on a trip to Moscow in 2007 to Alexander Tubelsky's memorial, Debbie and I had a marathon three hour discussion about this at a restaurant. In the end we found common ground and she has been a keynoter at three AERO conferences since then.

There have been some interesting learner-centered public alternatives in New York City. One, City as School, is a public high school with 500 students, in which the curriculum consists of internships in their fields of interest around the city. And there are several other ones with their own unique aspects; however, there are no actual democratic public schools that specifically empower students to make decisions about their school in the city.

Another interesting public school is The Met, in Providence, Rhode Island. One of the founders is Dennis Littky. His partner is Elliot Washor. Dennis has been a longtime public school gadfly. He's been fighting the system forever.

He was able to start this school in Providence, technically under the vocational school system, as part of the regular public school system. The idea of these vocational schools is that the maximum number of students is 100 and the emphasis is on internships. There seems to be a pretty good mixture of students.

A lot of the students' time is spent in internships, working in a field that interests them. They come into the school at various times during the week and work with multi-age advisory groups. Each student has an individual learning plan. They have a general meeting every week, one of which I sat in on. Their meeting starts with a group activity; they will sometimes have a speaker talk at the meeting, and they make decisions about the program.

When I went to the school, a couple of students were doing a presentation on a project they had organized, in which they had gone down south doing research on the Civil Rights Movement. They saw where Martin Luther King was killed, and they met James Meredith, who first integrated the schools down there.

The group had to do their own fundraising to be able to make the trip. They made a connection with a group from a college nearby and went on the tour with them. I watched their joint presentation with representatives from the college group, to parents, staff, and other students.

They put on a slide show and showed videos and it seemed an impressive project and a good example of some of the kinds of things that they're able to do at the Met. The Met now has funding from the Gates Foundation. As a result of the success of this first school, the directors have opened a second one, built two more in Providence and are opening at least eight more in Providence and other cities around the country. The book about the Met, called *One Kid at a Time*, was written by Eliot Levine, and is a good description of how the school works.

The number of Met Schools has exploded more recently and they are now spread all over the country and even in other countries. By 2008 there were over 60 Met schools in 14 states. They are all part of a nonprofit called Big Picture Learning. Dennis Littky wrote one of the chapters in our book, *Turning Points*.

When we were organizing Brooklyn Free School another committee actually wrote a nice proposal for a public democratic school in New York City. But I think the concept was too radical for them. AERO helped to start several independent democratic schools in the New York area. In addition to Brooklyn Free School there is Pono, in West Harlem, and the Agile Learning Center (formerly Manhattan Free School) in East Harlem. In Queens there is the Queens Paideia School, not a democratic school but a nice progressive school. And across the Hudson River in New Jersey there is the South Mountain Coop, a democratic school.

Meanwhile, when Debbie Meier got frustrated with

working in the city she went to direct the Mission Hill Elementary School in Boston—a public pilot school— and has since retired. One of the things that is interesting about her experience is that it shows how one school's ideas can at least spread to a district.

It also shows how difficult it is to put cracks in that system.

Chapter Twelve

International Work

Throughout its history, the Alternative Education Resource Organization has been involved with learner-centered education around the world, not only in the United States.

In 1989 while at a conference featuring Ivan Illich in Toronto, I read in a local newspaper about the Kee Way Win Tribe at Sandy Lake near the Ontario/Manitoba border. They had moved to their ancestral land that was not recognized by the Canadian government. Therefore they had no schools or help with housing, so their children were illiterate and people were living in tents in 30 below zero weather. They had no electricity and running water.

I managed to talk to the chief of the tribe who used a microwave phone powered by two car batteries. He asked me to come up there to help them start a school.

I took a train to Montreal, then another to Sioux Lookout, Ontario. From there I flew on Bearskin Airlines 200 miles away from the nearest road, landing on the frozen Sandy Lake. From there I went by skimobile 26 miles across the lake in 30 below temperature to their encampment.

I spent two weeks there and helped them start their school. Once it was started, by treaty the Canadian government had to recognize it. This eventually led to the community getting proper support. The school continues to this day. That was AERO's first major project, and the birth of the organization.

In those early years of AERO we forged relationships with people around the world that have lasted to this day. In August of 1990 Summerhill School brought me to a conference there to represent alternative education in the United States. I have been to the school more that 15 times since. Among other things we helped them get through their confrontation with the English education authorities in the late 1990s.

At another conference I met Roger Holdsworth of Australia who continues to promote the student voice in public schools.

I met Patrice Creve from France who helped start alternatives there. In 1996 we had a French-American summer camp in the Pyrenees Mountains.

I met leaders of the alternative school movement in West Germany when those schools were illegal.

Nellie Dick was 97 years old when she contacted me and introduced me to the Modern School Movement that was founded by Francisco Ferrer in Spain in the early 1900s. She had been a teacher in the Modern Schools. The schools were democratic and continued to run until 1958. But they have a reunion every year and I've been to most of them since I met Nelly, who lived to be 102.

We continued our relationship with the Mohawk Indians, in New York and Canada.

One of the most profound experiences I have had was when I visited Russia for the first time. I'm going to talk about this in some detail.

Back in 1991, I got a letter in the mail from Ron Miller. He forwarded a flyer to me announcing the first New Schools Festival of the Soviet Union. He said he couldn't go and wondered if I might be interested in going. At that point, the idea seemed completely preposterous.

I didn't know anything about the Soviet Union; it seemed like a forbidding place. Nobody really knew that there had been any kind of new or alternative schools in Russia. But the more I thought about it the more I realized that our new organization, AERO, should be doing just this kind of thing. We should be finding out about various kinds of alternatives that were out there and connecting people.

I got in touch with the woman in Holland, Ute Roehl, who was dealing with the festival-goers from Europe. At this time the only American who was going was Albert Lamb, who was working in England at Summerhill. Ute informed me about the rather complicated logistics that were involved. I had to get formal invitations, visas, and arrange transportation.

I didn't want to drop out of the sky into Russia. So I decided to fly to England and then take a train to Russia.

I got my visa, flew to England, took the ferry to Belgium, and the next day got on a train called the East West Express. It consisted of several cars that they would continue to attach and detach to one train or another until it got to Moscow. The East West Express was not fancy and few people on it spoke English.

I brought some food, but didn't realize that I probably should have brought a lot of food. There was no diner on the train. At one point I heard that on one of the

cars behind us there was a man who had come on with a
pushcart with food on it, several cars back. So I walked
back to find this guy and was able to pick up some drinks
and food.

When I got back to our car, the door was locked going
into the car. I looked through the window. We had been
stopped at a station platform, and our car had separated
from the car I was in and was pulling ahead. I jumped out
of the train and ran down the platform and caught up
with our train and managed to jump in the last door.

When I got to the border of Poland, to what was
then the edge of the Soviet Union, the size of the tracks
changed. I figured that the logical thing would be to have
us change trains. That was not what happened. Instead,
they jacked up the cars and changed all the wheels on the
entire train to adapt to the different size of the tracks.

I was told that Stalin had made the tracks smaller
on purpose, so he couldn't be attacked easily by train.
I managed to videotape a little of this process until they
came over and practically knocked the camera out of my
hands.

I continued on to Moscow and met Alexander
Tubelsky, from the School of Self-Determination, and
he showed the group around Moscow. Then we got on
another train and went down through Kharkov and the
Ukraine, where my mother's mother was born, and into
the Crimea to a town by the name of Simferipol. The
Crimea was the Florida of the Soviet Union. It was where
everyone went to get to the ocean, which in this case was
the Black Sea. This was now August, 1991, and it was very
warm.

There were 400 people at this conference and 70 children. The organizers understood that in order to have a good festival of New Schools, they needed to have the students there. It was a wonderful conference; I made all kinds of connections that continue to this day. As a result of that conference, communication was opened up between alternative schools in the former Soviet Union, Eastern Europe and the west. I met Alexander Adamsky and Elina Shepel who were from the Eureka Free University and were doing a teacher-training program to train teachers in alternative methods of education. I subsequently went to several of their training sessions with groups of people from the west.

And this is where I met people from the Stork Family School. Their school is in a town called Vinnitsa in the Ukraine. When they met me and discovered that my grandmother was born in the Ukraine, they considered me American only by accident of birth, and they adopted me into their family. I made a connection with the Stork School that couldn't be broken.

They even had me participate in a play they were putting on. It was kind of a political play based on the *Goose That Laid the Golden Egg*. They gave me some lines to memorize in Russian and when I spoke those lines, it brought down the house.

After the conference we went back to Moscow. At the station they wouldn't let me get on the train to go back to England because I hadn't reserved a specific day. I told them that we had been down in the Crimea and hadn't been able to do that. They said that maybe if I went down the next day and got in line, I might be able to book a ticket.

The next day I did just that, but I wasn't able to get a ticket, so I decided, "Well, I'm going to do this the American way. Let's go see the boss." Our translator came with me and we went to see the head of the railroad at the Moscow station. He said there was nothing he could do. We would need to give him several days' notice.

I told him that we were having a meeting later that day in President Boris Yeltsin's White House. He said, "In that case, we can put you first on the waiting list but you still have to call us later."

So we called him later from Yeltsin's White House. He said we should go down and get the tickets immediately. The White House dispatched a car for me, brought me to the station, and I got the ticket. The next day I got on the train and headed off to England.

Forty-five hours later, when I got to England, I discovered that where I had been standing in front of the Russian White House, just two days before, was where Yeltsin had just been, standing on a tank, to hold off the army troops attempting their failed coup.

Not long after that that there was no more Soviet Union.

In the following years I went to several conferences that were organized by Eureka Free University in Russia and the Stork School was also invited to a couple of them. So I continued to see the wonderful relationship that the students had with the teachers. A deep level of communication existed between them and they worked closely together at these conferences.

AERO continued to maintain a relationship with them all through those years but I had never actually been to the school until 1998, when the Stork Family School hosted the International Democratic Education Conference in Vinnitsa, Ukraine. During the years when they had financial crises, we were able to get funds to help them survive. At one point, the government was taking something like 80 percent of their tuition in taxes. They obviously were trying to discourage the existence of a private school. Finally, in January of 2001, I was invited to participate in the 10th anniversary celebration of the Stork School. Ten years later I went to the 20th. In 2015 they celebrated the 25th.

The school moved to its present location in a former state kindergarten several years ago. It is a sizable two-floor building. Now they have about 200 students, kindergarten through 12th Grade. They are divided up into different age and class levels. The school is broadly based in terms of arts and music and academics. They don't have a democratic process for the whole school, but they have done some experimenting with it, after learning more about it, and some of the individual classes now have a democratic process.

The students seem to love being there. They have a special museum, where a craftsman teaches the children how to do pottery work and clay work. They do weaving. They learn all kinds of music with an amazing music teacher who teaches them songs in many different languages. They learn to play many instruments and they seem also to do very well in science and math. One of the graduates is currently at the Russian equivalent of MIT.

Something they do that is unique is that they have a Montessori program option for younger children at the school. I don't know that I've ever seen another school that had a choice for parents of a Montessori or non-Montessori program.

They first heard about Montessori at that original First New Schools Festival. At that point there were no Montessori schools in all of the Soviet Union. That's just one example of the kind of flexibility that the Stork School has. I remember a funny story about that. When workers at the Festival were moving the heavy bags with Montessori materials they said, "Who the heck is this Montessori person who has so many heavy bags?"

It's hard to communicate the depth of caring of these people, the depth of their humanity, and their commitment to the school and to the children who are in the school. They've survived against incredible odds to keep the school going and it is a very bright light.

At one point they were selected to host the UNESCO Conference (United Nations Educational, Scientific and Cultural Organization). I think people are beginning to notice this school and how special it is. Going to the First New Schools Festival was the first opening between Western alternative and those in Eastern Europe.

As a result of those first visits to Russia and Ukraine we were able to connect with several other schools in Eastern Europe, such as the Rogers Person Centered School in Hungary, based on the work of psychologist Carl Rogers. In 1993 Yaacov Hecht, who had founded the Democratic School of Hadera, invited a few of us from democratic schools who has been at a multicultural conference in

Israel to a small meeting at his school. It included Dan Greenberg of Sudbury and David Gribble of Sands School in England. It was a nice meeting, but there was little indication that it would recur.

The next year David Gribble had another such meeting at Sands School. When I heard about that I thought, "Hmm, it's a movement!" It was the beginning of what eventually became the International Democratic Education Conference. Gribble put out a little newsletter about it for a few years, and in 1996 I created a listserv to network those interested in the democratic education conference and that has coordinated them since then.

The effect of these meetings has often been powerful. For example we had the conference at the Stork Family School in 1998 when the government was putting pressure on them and they backed off. We had the IDEC at Summerhill School when it was under attack in 1999. That helped their case against the government. We had the IDEC in Germany in 2005 when it was illegal to have a democratic school. The final day was at a prestigious university and that had a strong impact. Seven years later, at the IDEC back at Sands School, a third of the participants, well over 100, were from democratic schools in Germany! More recently, when we had the IDEC in Korea in 2014, the 200 illegal democratic schools in the country were threatened by the government. We organized protests on the streets of Seoul that were covered by national television. I was one of the people interviewed. The government has left them alone since.

Since 2006 we have had an online school starters course that runs from September to January. Through that and other means we have helped start over 100 alternative schools. Many have been on other countries. One of our school starters was from Poland. She took the course and also came to an AERO conference, then went back and started her school in Warsaw, Poland. That lit a spark there and there are now ten democratic schools in Poland. We've seen similar surprising participation in the course. For example we've had several people from Arab countries in the Middle East in the course and they are working hard to establish alternatives in their countries.

In 2015 I experienced something similar to the East/West opening when I went to Russia. In this case I was invited to be a keynote speaker at an alternative education conference in Bogota, Colombia, South America.

AERO has members all over the world but South America has been a relative blind spot, partly because of the language barrier. The person who invited me to keynote there is a film maker, German Doin Compos, who made the documentary La Educacion Prohibida, about alternative education in South America. He had persuaded the outgoing mayor of Bogota to sponsor a big conference.

It was an amazing event. I was the only native English speaker there. I discovered an emerging movement, still largely underground, to establish learner-centered education all over South America. We offered free AERO membership to all attendees. There were some very exciting and significant initiatives there. We hope to help and network them any way we can.

One relationship there illustrates the spirit of the event. I shared a taxi with a man who had founded a

Montessori School in Santiago, Chile. He really didn't speak any English and I barely spoke any Spanish, but we became good friends, using pantomime, gestures, a pocket translator and the few words we know. After the conference we Skyped and I even endorsed his new book! Luckily all of my presentations were translated at the conference.

My experience in Colombia underlined the fact that learner-centered education is taking root all over the world. As I've said, we've also seen it in Arab countries, but also in China, and Africa. In fact, the IDEC will be in Kenya in 2018. I'm hoping it gets to the point that we can barely keep up with tracking its growth. I think this is happening because it is a very reasonable response to thriving in this new millennium. People must become continual learners. They must be ready for sometimes drastic changes and they must become entrepreneurial.

I was happy that the trip was successful, as it was my first since suffering a heart attack during New Years Eve of 2015.

I had the heart attack at a table tennis league. Since I had angioplasty 19 years earlier, I knew what a heart attack would feel like, even though I hadn't had one. I said to my opponent, "I'm going to have to default—I'm having a heart attack!" I had someone drive me to the nearest hospital. Unfortunately they didn't have a catheter lab there, so they had to bring me to another hospital by ambulance. Within two and a half hours the cardiologist had removed "The biggest blood clot I ever removed from a heart." I had a 100% block of the "widowmaker" left anterior descending artery and put in a stent. And I had walked into the hospital!

I was out of the hospital in three days. I heard encouraging words from people in 25 countries. One of my readers sent a book to me by heart expert and nutritionist Dr. Joel Fuhrman. Since then I have followed his radical diet that is heavily based on nutrient dense leafy greens, is almost vegan, with no added oils, sugar, or salt, and no grains except for oatmeal. I've lost 30 pounds, back to my teenage weight, and I feel great. When I got the Fuhrman book I took it as a challenge. Now my cholesterol is so low on this diet I'm not taking any medications but a baby aspirin. I have unlimited energy again. But I did discover that it can all be over in a flash. And I did remember that my father, at age 75, played tennis, came home, took in the paper, then laid down on the couch and died.

Twenty years ago I had two angioplasties for 90 and 95% blockages in my heart. This rupture of the plaque was at the same spot. A few days after the second one I had some pain in the middle of the night and wrote this free verse:

> And then one morning you don't wake up.
> Everyone says how surprised they were.
> You would have been the most surprised.
> But NOTHING surprises you any more!

On October 14th, 2016 I participated in a panel of alumni at my old public high school, speaking to the current high school seniors. Actually I wasn't expecting much.

There was a lineup of about a dozen alumni graduating as little as seven years ago to as much as 55 years ago, speaking one after the other for five or six minutes each. But as they spoke an important theme emerged. Over and over again they told stories of their search for meaningful work. Some felt they had been misdirected by expectations. Some started out in one direction only to discover it wasn't what they wanted to do.

The clear theme was "Find your passion!" A couple of the younger ones are now in the business of making apps. But several pointed out that they must be entrepreneurial and that the field they might go into probably doesn't even exist yet. Someone else said that whatever you think you are going to do now, the chances of that becoming your final vocation may be 10%. Therefore you need to be able to continuously learn and change direction.

There was a lawyer who became a musician, and then became a judge. There was writer who became a farmer. There was an athlete who found his passion in volunteering.

There were about 100 seniors in the audience. When I spoke I pointed out the theme of finding your passion and the need for learner-centered education. I also mentioned that my grandfather used to sit down with me when I was six or seven and ask me "What do you want to learn?" That seemed to me the obvious way to become educated. But when I discovered that most schools don't work that way I became a rebel and continue to be one! I once called my high school "The best school of a failed system!" That's when I wrote the poem which I reprinted at the beginning of this book.

As I've mentioned, when I was fifteen I organized my friends into a study group that could discuss and explore anything. We even had our own guest speakers when we couldn't find the answers ourselves.

My point was underlined when a bell rang during the panel and half the seniors stood up and had to leave. As John Gatto points out, that phenomenon underlines that idea that no learning is important and anything can be cut short by a bell, forcing you to go elsewhere.

There is an alternative within the school call School Within a School, or SWS. It has been going since 1971 and runs democratically. I have heard that the democratic school I had started three years earlier inspired it. After the panel a student from SWS came up to me and she said she was studying educational alternatives and wanted to get involved with AERO and be part of our next conference. There is hope!

Chapter Thirteen

The System and the Future

There is no good way to predict the future of education. One of the last times I tried was when I predicted in 1999 that the No Child Left Behind/High Stakes Testing phenomenon would be short lived, a year or two, as was the Back to Basics Movement. Unfortunately I was quite wrong. That process ground on and on feeding on itself and the massive development of the testing industry. At this writing it seems that things may be finally changing. Here on Long Island the Opt-Out Movement, parents and their children refusing to take the high stakes tests, seems to have become one of the most massive examples of civil disobedience in United States history. In 2015 half of Long Islanders refused to have their children subjected to these tests; over 200,000 people total in New York State. In 2016 the government pretended to listen and put off some elements in their regime for a few years, but the public was not fooled. Even more opted out that year. What might bring these families to the next step? When will they begin opting out of schools that oppress their children or insisting that their schools adjust to the new millennium and become democratic and learner-centered?

There is some justification for looking into the possibility of actually franchising something, so that there is a procedure to follow to set up a successful democratic meeting even for a school that doesn't necessarily get founded by such a charismatic leader. It sounds like an oxymoron, a bit like the ironic fact that freedom often needs to be very structured to work well. Maybe we should be thinking more about a structure that anybody could follow. Sudbury Valley School is already doing this successfully by offering people their school-starting kits. AERO has now had ten years of successful school starter courses and has helped start over 100 schools and programs. But in the big picture that is just a drop in the bucket.

Maybe we need to look at this in a broader sense. I've thought that there needs to be a charter school organization that can help people who want to create a democratic charter school, something to compete with the corporate charters. Even though charters have become very skewed toward operating more like public schools, we shouldn't give up on them quite yet. We need people who are passionate and determined, ready to put time and energy and effort into seeing where we can make change.

The goal is for parents and students to have real choice and not to feel trapped into having to go to their local designated school. Options can include everything from Montessori schools, to Waldorf, to charter schools and magnet schools, higher education alternatives, homeschooling, public choice and public at-risk alternatives, free schools, outdoor schools and of course independent private schools. This wide spectrum is part of the strength of the alternative school movement.

There is also no doubt that the movement is growing. Some of the largest areas of growth include the charter schools and homeschooling. If the trajectory holds, at some time in the future we hope they will no longer be alternative, but the mainstream. The traditional system has been out of date for a long time and simply maintains itself in a familiar shape out of inertia. Their approach is so out of step with what is needed in the information age that they can't last much longer.

I was once asked if I could think of one thing to change in school that would make a key difference. I answered that we could leave the door open, so that students could go out or in as they chose. That freedom would change the nature of all schools; the learning would then be by choice. The teachers would have to listen to the children and their needs or they would have no students in their classroom. We need to create a new world in which adults know how to listen to children and to respect them as legitimate human beings. Developing the ability to listen to young people is crucial. It is time to open the door, a gateway to learning, based on the interest of the student.

Epilogue

There are so many wonderful examples of democratic schools and alternative thinkers. The schools have been transformative for both the movement and people's lives, and the individuals involved have changed the course of education in the United States and worldwide.

Democratic Schools

Sudbury Valley is one of the most important democratic schools in America, inspiring many people to start schools based on their model. They have a resource pack and program for people who want to start new schools and they publish many of their own books. Sudbury Valley has pioneered a process of self-examination that is providing us with our first scientific evidence about what happens to children who grow up in a democratic school. A visit to their website can really give you the best introduction to their unique way of doing things.

A while back they decided to grow bigger and they now have over 150 students. There was a feeling that their students could benefit from a large number of peers at every age level.

The community at Sudbury Valley has control over

every aspect of school life. Their meetings are more formal than the Summerhill meetings. When I visited Sudbury Valley the people did not sit in a circle, but in rows of chairs, sort of the way a New England town meeting operates. They use Robert's Rules of Order to manage their meetings.

Sudbury Valley has a Judicial Committee that meets nearly every school day to deal with people who are accused of various infractions. I sat in on one of these. Students come in and are questioned by members of the committee and the committee votes on what they think the consequences should be or whether they agree that the school law was broken or not. Summerhill used a similar system for a long time until they changed in 2002. At Sudbury Valley, the meeting makes the laws and there is an appeal process. The school has received a lot of media coverage.

*****

Grassroots Free School, in Tallahassee, Florida, has a meeting they call a "powwow." Although the founder, Pat Seery, spent some time at Summerhill, the school is also influenced by Indian decision-making methods. They have non-compulsory class attendance. I have visited them in two locations.

They are now located within an intentional community which they established. They moved a former African American church and a couple of other buildings to the property for the school.

I think the original thought was that a number of

parents living in the intentional community that was surrounding it would have their children going to the school, but that is not really the case any more, which creates an interesting situation.

Grassroots has students from kindergarten through high school, but generally when they get to be high school age they don't stay there. Some do, but for the most part they seem to go on to SAIL School, which is a public alternative that Seery helped to establish. One of the impressive things about Seery was that he always encouraged anybody in the Tallahassee area who wanted to start an alternative to do so and has felt that his school would still survive somehow. He helped start SAIL School and one or two others. He even hosted the initial meetings to help establish a charter school in the area.

One day when I visited, all of the staff had the flu. It struck me that there was really almost no difference between how the school was running with no staff and how it ran with staff. The students organized their various clubs and groups. Recreational games were organized. Students were working in the library and in classrooms on different projects. They were not at all dependent on the staff organizing things for them. Anyone at Grassroots can call a powwow anytime they want.

*****

The Greenbrier School was established as a day school on a large piece of property about 45 minutes from Austin, Texas. The school used to take a bus into Austin, pick up children, bring them to the school, have school, and bus them home. Gradually people began to come out to the land and build structures there to live in. At a certain point, they stopped sending the bus out.

Greenbrier has had up to 100 students, but the last time I visited there were about 50 people living in the community and 25 children. The way it has evolved, it's almost like a giant homeschool. Everybody is there for the students.

It is still legally a school, not just a community, and is accredited. They occasionally have children come in as day school students, but generally speaking everybody in the school lives there. I saw wonderful scenes in people's houses, all kinds of classes and one-on-one's with adults. Somebody would be doing a book report in one corner and someone else would be doing driver's education in another.

They have a shop, a trampoline, and a swimming pool. They do have a main school building, but things can take place anywhere in the community. In fact, they think of themselves as somewhat of an anarchist community. They all get together and make decisions democratically. Everyone who lives there gets to be involved in the decision-making. As far as I know, no outside teachers are hired. They've been around since the early '70s. One side note: Dave Lehman, one of the premier public educators, who founded Alternative Community School in Ithaca, NY, was one of the founders of Greenbrier. He has now retired and the Alternative Community School has been renamed after him, The Lehman Alternative School.

*****

The Arthur Morgan School, was founded by the daughter-in-law of Arthur Morgan, the man who started the progressive Antioch School in the early 1920s. Later, he was instrumental in radicalizing Antioch College. Arthur's son, Ernest Morgan, died on October 29, 2000, in his nineties. He had helped keep the school going for all these years.

The Arthur Morgan School is the only boarding alternative junior high school in the country. No other group seems to be foolish enough to try to tackle that age, and only that age.

The school has 500 acres in an extremely beautiful area in Burnsville, North Carolina. They make decisions by consensus and have required class attendance. The students get to do a fair amount of traveling. They have had major field trips where they have gone and worked, for example, in migratory worker camps. This is a good example of schools outliving their original founders and thriving.

*****

Harmony School is in Bloomington, Indiana. Some of the founders of the school are still there, including Steve Bonchek. The school was founded in 1974. It kept moving until about the early '90s when Steve negotiated an arrangement with the local public school. They were able to buy a former public school building for a symbolic $10. The story they tell is that every child who planned to be going to the school came in with a dime. At the time there were about 100 students.

Now, there are 200 or so. One of the special things about this school is that they do a lot of local fundraising and so even though it's a private school, they have a sliding scale and will take in students regardless of how little money their family has.

They do have compulsory class attendance, but they also have a democratic meeting. I went there one time and I had quite a debate with the students about whether or not they should have compulsory classes. One student said to me, "Well, if I didn't have to go to class I would just sit home watching television and smoking all day." I remember his teachers being shocked at that statement— to think that their students really thought that if they were not forced to go to classes they wouldn't be going! But the students certainly seem to love the school. It's a K-12 school and they take quite an interesting variety of students.

Harmony School has actually become a hub for some other projects that are related to democratic education. They do consulting at other schools. Daniel Baron, one of the staff members, runs a program in which he goes into other schools around the country and helps them with democratic process.

*****

Jefferson County Open School is one of the more interesting public alternatives in the US, founded by Arnie Langberg. He had started a public alternative on Long Island, The Village School in Great Neck before he went out to the Denver area. First, in Denver, he was the founding principal of a program called Mountain Open, then another program for younger children called Tanglewood. These programs were later merged into the Jefferson County Open School.

The setup for the older children still seems radical. They encourage the children to go anywhere they would like to go. When I was there I heard a report from a group of children about a canoe trip they had made up in Canada. There was also a girl who had gone down to a biological research laboratory in Louisiana.

They have a democratic process for their 600 students and a democratic meeting for the older children. They use a system of advisory groups. Each child has an advisor, who meets with them individually but also in a group setting.

The last time I visited, it happened to be the day of the Columbine massacre. A number of us had gone to a conference of the National Coalition of Alternative Community Schools that was held near Denver, where Jefferson County is.

By prearrangement, the students from the Albany Free School had planned to stay in the Jefferson County gym. At that point, all the other schools in Denver were closed as a result of the massacre and people were very worried about the situation. Out of concern for their security our children were actually locked in the building and there were guards around. If they wanted to leave the building for any purpose they had to contact the security people and let them know that the door was going to be opened.

I interviewed Arnie Langberg on my national radio show the night of Columbine and I talked to him about his school and the nearby Columbine High School, which actually had a number of former Jefferson County students going there at the time. I asked him if something like this could have happened in his school and he said no, they might have had a couple of children that were that crazy, but because of the degree and depth of communication in his school, they would find out about it. Arnie felt that this kind of thing could not have happened at Jefferson County because people would have gone to see what these students were up to.

*****

North Star Center, which used to be called Pathfinder School, is in Hadley, Massachusetts. It was originally the idea of Josh Hornick, and Ken Danford. They tried to get funding for a radical charter school in which students would have a lot of freedom to study what they wanted. Their proposal for a charter school was not funded so they decided to set this up as an educational program for homeschoolers instead.

The idea originally was that students could come in anytime they wanted and classes would be organized for them. Since they were homeschoolers, no set curriculum was imposed. The basic educational responsibility was still taken by the parents. After a while many of the homeschoolers drifted away and then people started contacting North Star, saying they wanted their children to go to the school.

The staff pointed out that it was not a school and that for students to go there they would have to become homeschoolers. Josh estimates that 85% of the students going there now are from families who came to them originally and had to be helped through the process of becoming homeschoolers. They usually have more than 60 students.

When I visited them the last time they were in a very pleasant space but have since moved to another one. They have meetings with all of the students and classes that are scheduled. Students can also ask for classes if they want or they can hang out with each other. It is an opportunity for those who are technically homeschooling to be able to socialize and to have control of their education.

I think this is significant for a number of reasons: This is a way that homeschooling can grow beyond the usual model of a parent teaching their children at home. Parents, when they're homeschooling, have the right to hire whoever they want to do the teaching of their children even though they still take the legal responsibility.

The current homeschool system is limited mostly to two parent families in which one can stay at home, or to people who have home businesses. It can expand from that if parents start using homeschool resource centers. A number of similar centers are popping up all around the United States. Northstar has a program to help people start similar centers.

*****

In 2003, AERO and Albany Free School co-hosted the International Democratic Education Conference in Troy, NY. It was an amazing gathering with over 600 attendees from 28 countries, including a hundred from developing countries. There were 17 keynotes over 8 days.

On the way back to New York City, a group of educators wondered why there were no democratic schools there. So we began to have a series of meetings at the Renaissance Charter School in Queens. We established two committees: one created an elegant proposal for a public democratic school in New York City, the other worked on establishing an independent democratic school.

One of the participants in the latter group, Alan Berger, had contacted us about the idea of having a democratic school and we invited him to the group. We had many meetings, eventually getting together every two weeks or so in a different Brooklyn apartment. At these meetings we demonstrated organic curriculum and democratic decision making.

We always encouraged people to bring their children to the meetings. Parents brought three 6-year-olds to one of the meetings, but they ran off to play amongst themselves. At the meeting I pointed out that these students should be involved with discussions about the future school, that I was sure they had opinions about it.

So we invited them into the meeting. When one of them realized that we knew he had opinions about the proposed school, he admonished us: "It's very important that the school not be too clean or have too much nice furniture. If it does we won't be able to really run around and play the way we want to!" Only a 6-year-old could have understood that!

At another meeting, the group was trying to decide

what should be the lowest age of student and by what age they could participate in a meeting. They started a discussion about the age at which students should be able to leave the school to go to the store. A 10-year-old, though it could be 7 or 8. We then invited a 4-year-old into the meeting. Upon understanding the issue he said, "You know, there's trucks out there and busses. I don't think they should be able to go until they are 10!" The school now takes students four and up!

The group established Brooklyn Free School which opened in 2004 with Alan Berger as Director. It opened with 35 students in a church in Park Slope. After six years it was able to buy its own building in the Clinton Hill area. It has a sliding scale tuition, so many of the students are minority and low income. As of 2016, it was operating with 80 students. It is a democratic school with non-compulsory class attendance.

By the way, the proposal for the public democratic school sat on a bureaucrat's desk until we insisted on having a meeting with New York City Public School officials. The concept was too radical for them.

*****

The School of Self-Determination was started by Alexander Tubelsky as an experimental school in inner-city Moscow. It has always been part of the regular public school system. They have 600 students from pre-kindergarten through 12th Grade.

The school has a parliament that makes basic decisions about how the school runs. The students have a constitution with specific rights. One of those rights is to leave any class whenever they want without explanation, the same as any adult would be able to do.

When prospective teachers come into the school, they give sample lessons to the students and then the students vote on which teachers are going to be hired. This is the kind of thing that couldn't happen in any public school in the United States that I know of.

Also, within this school, there was a special program called Park Schooling or the Park School, which is based on the ideas of Miloslav Balaban. His daughter, Olga, organized this program within the School of Self-Determination and ran it for over five years. The concept is to see the school as if you were going into a park and could do anything you chose. The 70 students in this program were able to use any of the school facilities as they saw fit; for example, they could go teach a class of younger students, they could work in any of the studios they wanted—woodworking, sewing, weaving—they could do plays, and they could work independently. This program was very successful. Although Olga left and the program stopped, it was a stunning example of what could be done in a public school. Olga is still working to create more such programs in Russia.

Alexander Tubelsky, who died in 2007, was a professional actor before he went into education and you can see this by the way he interacted with students. I've brought American students with me to visit his school and when they have been in the same room with Tubelsky, as he was speaking they were in absolutely rapt attention, just fascinated by the way he expresses himself, even though they couldn't understand a word of Russian.

A good friend of mine, Alla Denesenko, was a teacher in the school and the head of the foreign language department and she worked very closely with Tubelsky in the early years, several years before the coup, when they were setting up this school. It came about as part of Glasnost.

Alla said they went into an existing public school, took it over, and then had to make their radical changes in that school, something that's incredibly difficult to do. Alla talks in detail about the trials and tribulations they went through during this rough period during which the teachers were questioning the approach that Tubelsky was taking with the students. But the school became very successful and transitioned to one of his proteges.

In their school parliament they elect representatives. It would be pretty difficult to have a meeting with a school of 600 people. Not impossible, but I don't know that they have any place that would hold such a large number. The representatives make the decisions with the teachers.

One concern I had about the school is that Tubelsky subscribed to a view that is common in Russia, something called "Author's Schools." The concept behind them is that these schools are something like works of art by a particular leader. The problem with that concept is that each school is unique and not replicable. However this does go along with my idea that these schools must first be run by charismatic democratic leaders who can empower students. The fact that it did make a transition is significant.

*****

When I first visited the Democratic School of Hadera, they were hosting the International Democratic Education Conference in Israel. They have 300 students and at the time they had 3000 on their waiting list. The school is in Hadera, Israel, north of Tel Aviv, and has a big open campus area with a bunch of buildings in a square with a great big open area in the middle where they sometimes played soccer. They have classrooms, a library, music room, art rooms, and outside play equipment. It's a kindergarten through 12th grade school. Recently they have built new buildings. I haven't seen that and hope they have retained the unique feel. I know they were aware of the challenge.

What disturbed me about the situation when I first visited is that homeschooling is illegal in Israel, or was at the time. With so many on the waiting list it seemed almost unconscionable that the ones who couldn't go there couldn't be homeschooling. This has been somewhat rectified by the person who was then the director of the school, Yaacov Hecht. He helped establish over 25 more democratic schools with government money, since that time, and more are being established. He also helped create a university program for training teachers to teach in democratic schools.

Yaacov is an amazingly dynamic man who has a clear vision of children being natural learners. He describes himself as a dyslexic and is very self-deprecating when he talks. But he's a brilliant speaker.

There is a parliament at the school that makes decisions, but again, it seems that the room for the parliament is hardly big enough for 300 people to sit in there so I wonder what happens when they have a really hot issue. They also have a separate judicial system for people who break the rules of the school. The staff lean toward the Sudbury model of having no scheduled classes, but they have a vote about this every year and every year the students vote that they want to have scheduled classes. So that's the way it seems to continue.

There have been quite an interesting variety of schools established that have been modeled from the Democratic School of Hadera. One of them was started recently by Moshe Lerner. It combines religious and nonreligious students and it's quite innovative.

Few schools in Israel bring Jews and Arabs together, but there was one wonderful school that Yaacov described that was in a very poor area of Tel Aviv. They had a large building so they were able to do some innovative things. They had about one third fairly poor Jewish families who couldn't afford to move out of the area, one third Arabs, and about one third foreign workers who have come into the country. It used to have the very lowest test scores in all of Tel Aviv.

They made the school experiential. They brought in a number of interesting people who had workshops or offices in the school building, on the condition that they provide learning experiences and internships for the students in the school. They even had a circus that had its home base in the basement. There were legal offices and craftsmen who operated out of the school. All of these people provided learning experiences for the children. I'm not sure it still exists but it was a great example of what could be done in a public school.

A survey was done of all the schools around Tel Aviv and the students that liked their school the most were the ones from this school. They also had the greatest jump in their rate of learning of any school in the city, according to the standardized tests. There is also a democratic school in the Golan Heights and several others around the country.

Yaacov told us the story of one boy who was doing poorly in his school when they decided to send him to the Democratic School of Hadera. He was only interested in wind surfing. So Yaacov said to him that his entire curriculum would be based on wind-surfing: how to build them, sail them, studying weather, athletes, etc. Eventually he won the only gold medal Israel has ever won in the Olympics—in windsurfing!

One interesting experiment that Yaacov was working on at the time was taking an entire town of 5,000 people in the desert and making it into a learning community. Everyone living there was available educationally to other people in the community. This has been so successful that the town actually grew very rapidly with a lot of people from different parts of Israel moving in. This led to Yaacov's current project, working with mayors to create Education Cities.

These innovations that have grown out of the Democratic School of Hadera, and are continuing to be fomented by Yaacov Hecht, are very impressive and important.

*****

Sands School is in Ashburton, a small town in the beautiful English coastal county of Devon. Three teachers who had worked together at Dartington Hall started it. Dartington was one of the oldest and most famous radical boarding schools in England. When it closed, about 25 or so years ago, three of the staff members, David Gribble, Sybilla Higgs and Sean Bellamy, got together to set up a day school, Sands.

Sands is in a big old house with couple of acres of land behind it, right on the main street that goes through Ashburton. A block away is a swimming pool and they have tennis and basketball courts in the backyard. There are some gardens and a climbing wall. They have one outbuilding that is an art building and another one that is for woodworking. Seventy students attend now, which is about as big as it's been. When I visited at first it had only about 35 students and they were worrying about whether the school could be sustained.

Sands runs as a democracy with non-compulsory class attendance. One of the significant things about Sands is that it's a day school. So whereas Summerhill can draw its students from all over the world, Sands has to find its them locally. They seem to have been able to do that, and also some people have moved to the area so their children could go to the school. They even have a few who are living with other families so that they can attend. Students' ages range from 11 to 16.

Sands School has an admissions committee that

decides who can get in. I've sat in on one admissions committee meeting, which was comprised almost entirely of students. Their democratic meeting process has gotten better and better over the years. In fact, the day I last visited the meeting was all students. The staff member who was supposed to be there couldn't make it. They take their meeting very seriously.

There are some disadvantages to being just a day school and not having any young students. But Sands is successful, very strong, and has a very stable staff. Some of the staff and students have participated in the International Democratic Education Conferences from the beginning.

In 1996, the Sands School hosted the IDEC and two Sands students, two girls of about 16 years old, organized it. Before the event I was frustrated because I couldn't find out what was scheduled for that IDEC and I finally called Sean Bellamy, the director of the school, and asked him what was going on. He didn't know, because these two students really were organizing the conference themselves!

I eventually discovered that their purpose was to have everybody come to the conference and have the conference co-created on the spot with all the participants, and with particular emphasis on the student input. They felt that to do otherwise would have been to create a typical talking head conference that inevitably would have been adult oriented. It was also designed to last for ten days because they felt the group should become a mini-community instead of coming together for a quick conference and then dispersing.

Their conference, although relatively small, with only

about 80 participants, was very successful. It included activities like hiking into the moors, caving, swimming and other things that might not have been scheduled had it been organized entirely by adults. There was also a game there that was being promoted by one of the students called tamborelli, which is sort of a racket game in which you use a tambourine to hit the birdie with. And, in fact, there were still the usual talking-head presentations, so it was a mixture of workshops. It was one of the most interesting conferences I've been to. This IDEC set many precedents that have echoed down the years. First, they actually named it the International Democratic Education Conference. They started the open setting for workshops, and set the meeting in the summer so it could be longer. These traditions have continued for the next 19 years, with IDECs in Ukraine, Japan, Australia, India, the United States (the one we hosted), Brazil, Korea, Puerto Rico, and Finland. I've been to 18 of the 21 official ones.

Alternative Thinkers

John Holt was one of the leading writers of our movement. He wrote effective critiques of conventional education and encouraged people to start alternative schools. He had been writing books on education since the early 1960s, including his bestseller *How Children Fail* and its companion, *How Children Learn*. In the late '70s he gave up on the idea of schools and wrote a book called *Teach Your Own*. That was one of the beginnings of the homeschool movement, growing out of the alternative school movement.

I first met John Holt around 1967. I was not in school anymore, but I met him when he was speaking at Goddard College. I was teaching at one of the regular schools I taught at before I started Shaker Mountain. After his talk I said to him that I wanted to get a job at an alternative school somewhere. So he took down some information about me.

Not long after that, I got a letter from John Holt asking me if I had found an alternative school to teach in. This to me was amazing, that he would follow up on all of these things. I wrote back to him and told him I had started a school, whereupon John Holt immediately put us on his list of endorsed alternative schools. This was very important to us because we then had all kinds of people who knew about us and who would contact us, wanting to teach at the school or support it. This started a communication I had with John over a long period of time. At that point he was still in his mode of being critical of schools and promoting alternative education. Whenever I would get down to the Boston area I would stop by and visit him.

After a while he soured on the whole idea of schools and started his *Growing Without Schooling* magazine, which led to the *Teach Your Own* book. I stopped in his office and had a discussion with him there and he was skeptical that any children would want to go to any school if they weren't forced to go. I had all I could do to try to convince him that Shaker Mountain was exceptional, that this was a school in which children were not required to go to classes and in which they tried to have school even when we had vacations. He did allow the possibility that such a school could exist, a school that children would want to go to even if they weren't forced.

Later on we invited John Holt to come to Vermont as a speaker at the local auditorium. We invited alternative schools and homeschoolers from all over the state to come and John drew quite a big audience. Out of this we put together the first organization for homeschoolers in Vermont.

John stayed overnight at our emergency shelter in Burlington. He was staying in our best room, which was the director's room, and that's where the phone was. At one point the phone rang and it was a teenager who had run away but wanted to come back. We were talking to him on the phone and started to take the phone out of the room and John sat straight up and said, "Oh no, please don't take the phone out of the room!" He wanted to hear the whole conversation and was very interested in what we were doing. Of course, the boy did come back. We didn't have many who ran away from that shelter.

I saw John for the last time, before his early death, when he spoke at the NCACS Conference in 1985 at Clonlara School in Michigan.

Someone asked him a question about the problems of fundamentalist Christian homeschoolers who try to do a kind of rigid school at home. He said he felt that over time either the children would teach the parents how to teach them or the parents would give up and just put them in a Christian school. I think time has tended to bear that out. Now the whole idea about the line between religious homeschooling and unschooling is blurred. There are many religious homeschoolers that liberally quote John

Holt and are basically unschoolers. His prediction in that respect was accurate.

I do occasionally think about John Holt and the way he did his work as being in some ways a role model for what we're doing at AERO. Our vision and goal always has been that if we could really unite this movement, we could have a significant impact on the education system and move the whole system in the direction of a learner-centered approach, one that really respected the needs and the rights of students.

AERO has the lonely task of trying to get people from these different types of alternatives to be aware of the other alternatives and to provide support and resources to people who are trying to provide a generally learner-centered approach in education. A few other people, besides John Holt, have done similar things; one was Len Solo who played a similar role with his Teacher Dropout Center in Massachusetts. Len Solo went on to run the Cambridge Alternative Public School and then, from 1983 to 2001, Cambridge's Graham and Parks School. AERO published his book in 2014, *Education: Back to the Future*.

*****

Another excellent writer on education was Jonathon Kozol, who had been a substitute teacher in the Boston public schools when he was young. He didn't teach for long but he wrote a book about it, the bestseller *Death at an Early Age* about the life of minority public school children in the Boston system, and then he continued to write about alternative schools.

Kozol wrote a book called *Free Schools*. One of the lines in his book caught the attention of someone on my staff. It was something to the effect that he cared about schools that worked with poor children and inner city children and minority children and not schools like those out in the country up in Vermont. Alan Boutillier, a Shaker Mountain staff member, wrote to Kozol and said it was time he learned something about schools up in Vermont. Boutillier said that we had a school that worked with mostly low-income students, and some inner city children and welfare children and he said that he took great exception to what he wrote. Kozol wrote back and apologized for that and said he would like to find out more about us. He actually got us a couple of hundred dollars through something called the New Nations Seed Fund.

Then around 1974 he invited me to a meeting in Boston at which they were going to try to create a national organization of alternative schools. There were only a dozen of us who went to that meeting in the basement of a church. Some of the others included Mary Leue of The Free School in Albany, and Dave Lehman, who later was principal at the Alternative Community School in Ithaca. Dave, at the time, was still busy editing the New Schools Exchange Newsletter, one of the early networking newsletters for alternative schools. My friend Greg Packan from Shaker Mountain, who was a lawyer, was also there.

We had this long discussion—I remember Kozol was sick; he had the flu or something. At that point he seemed to be espousing a philosophy that was pretty much extreme left in orientation. One of the discussions we had was questioning whether public schools should be allowed into this new coalition. Kozol was very much against it. He thought that public schools were part of a sort of state conspiracy and he kept using words like "proletariat" and so on. Both Mary and I said, "Look, this kind of language isn't going to wash in our communities." We were advocating being more inclusive.

A couple of years later Kozol, with some other people—one of them was Jack West—organized the first National Coalition of Alternative Community Schools meeting. They had quite a turnout and as a result, Jack Wuest eventually set up something called the Alternative Schools Network in Chicago, which continues to this day.

For a couple of years after that meeting there were no more meetings. Pat Montgomery, of Clonlara, started contacting people asking what happened to the NCACS. They resurrected it and had another meeting. This was around 1980. I went to my first NCACS meeting in 1982 in Chicago.

Some time later I saw Kozol at a conference that was organized by Jesse Jackson in Washington, DC in 2000. The opening was at the National Press Corp and he was one of the one or two featured speakers. I talked to him after that and gave him a copy of our magazine. He, of course, has made quite a name for himself over the years writing about children and minorities and the public schools. One of his latest books is called *Savage Inequalities*. I've always thought it was somewhat ironic that he has become the champion of what can be done and what ought to be done for the public school system whereas back in that meeting in the '70s he didn't even want public schools to be part of the coalition he was going to set up. The NCACS lasted until 2014.

*****

George Dennison was primarily a writer but in New York City he set up a school called The First Street School that had a lot of low-income students. He wrote a wonderful book called *The Lives of Children* about the way these children responded to the school situation. That became an important early book in the movement.

In a related story, at this time I had just started my school and there was a local religious ecumenical organization in the same town. I had gone to them originally to see if I could get their support for Shaker Mountain. We talked about the way we wanted to run the school, and the children who were going to be in it and so on. They expressed quite a bit of interest in what we were doing and the philosophy of it.

I went to them a couple of times for support but I didn't hear from them. Then one day I talked to a student that I knew and she said, "Oh, I've got to go to my free school now."

I said, "Your what?"

And she said, "Yes, yes, we started a new school." It had been started by that same ecumenical organization.

I asked who was in it and it was interesting: they were middle class students. I contacted them and asked what happened; we had asked them for support and then they had started a school in competition with ours. They said they took what we told them very seriously and called some students together they knew to discuss what we had said. Lo and behold, they said they wanted something like this too. So rather than contact us and support us and get the students into our school—with mostly low-income children—they set up a middle class alternative to what we were doing!

This is a painful lesson that I learned about liberals: these people were oblivious about what they had done. To them, it was all just a natural consequence: they asked the students and they wanted to do something and there it was. They were totally unconscious about how it might affect our school.

A little later, I heard through the people that I knew that George Dennison was coming to town to see the new free school. So I arranged to be there when he came. I introduced myself to him after his talk and told him about what we were doing and he was very interested. He went out to dinner with us afterwards. He came over to our school and stayed overnight with us . He said that he was sure that the middle class alternative school couldn't survive; liberals didn't have the guts to do it. But he was interested in what we were doing and totally supportive of it.

Some time after that I had a group of students who went on a trip with me to Maine and Nova Scotia. We were on our way to visit a school in New Brunswick called School in the Barn. It was an early alternative school. On the way we stopped to visit and stayed overnight at George Dennison's house and met his wife Mabel. Not too long after that he died. We were in touch with Mabel for many years after that time. She was involved with an alternative school in Maine.

*****

Edgar Z. Friedenberg was an important pioneer writer in education and one of his most important books was *The Vanishing Adolescent.* I gather that in protest of the Vietnam War he moved to Canada and he stayed there. I got the sense talking to him that in some respects he regretted that.

I was in communication with him and he invited me to come up to speak at Delhausie University in Halifax, Nova Scotia. This was in the late '70s. I went with two of my students by train to Montreal and from there to Nova Scotia and we stayed with Edgar for a few days. I spoke at his school. His house was a little ways away from Halifax, on the ocean.

He was living alone but he had a husky, a dog by the name of Sespe. Sespe was treated as if he were human by Edgar. He was a very smart dog. He could pick up things that you said just conversationally. For example, if Edgar said, "Well, maybe we'll take a walk out along the beach," in a conversational tone, the dog would jump up and down in excitement because he understood exactly what had been said.

Once when Edgar was out of the house Sespe seemed irritated and upset. We found a little food to try to feed him. He clearly didn't care about the food, didn't want to be petted, and was making strange sounds, kind of whining like wa-wa-wa. After a while, I got the feeling that the dog was actually trying to talk to us. I listened to him one more time and it sounded as if maybe somebody who couldn't speak properly was trying to say, "Where's Edgar?" So I said to the dog, "Did you say, 'Where's Edgar?" And Sespe said, "Wa." I said, "He's gone out to the chalet to do some work." At which point the dog calmly walked over to the door and waited to be let out. We opened the door, and he went down to the chalet.

Someone told me that Edgar died and that Sespe also died shortly after. I'm sorry I never stayed in contact with Edgar because he seemed an interesting and nice guy.

*****

Mary Leue was the founder of The Free School of Albany, New York, one of America's oldest and most innovative democratic schools. She started out because she needed something for her own children who were not happy in school. That grew into what became The Free School. I think in many ways she is a genius.

She hasn't been a writer in the same way as these other thinkers, but she has been an important editor. Her quirky and independent Skole magazine was for many years a real beacon to the alternative school movement. Mary managed to publish many of the most interesting stories to come out of the recent resurgence of democratic schools. She is now 95 years old as of this writing and has long since retired.

One of her most important early acts, influenced by Jonathon Kozol, was her decision not to try to base the income for the school on tuition but rather to start a business to support it. The business was buying up row houses in inner-city Albany and fixing them up. The income they make helps run the school.

The school has always run as a democracy, with quite young children, and the students have a fair amount of freedom. The Free School has found many unique ways, over the years, to interact with their inner-city community and to create a strong sense of community amongst themselves.

The meetings at The Free School in Albany are called council meetings because they are based on an Indian approach and were not just a pure democracy.

After we got to know each other in the early '70s, we had quite a bit of reciprocal visitation. We influenced each other. Mary says that the fact that we had a boarding location influenced her to do whatever she could to get the children out of Albany and over to her farm in the Berkshires, spending some time away from home.

Mary is a strong character, as you have to be to keep something like that going and thriving. She sometimes has a temper and often over the years she would get mad at me and slam down the phone and I would just pick it up and call her back again and we'd continue our conversation. So she knew I wasn't intimidated by her and that's been an important part of our relationship. I consider Mary to be one of my best friends and she's been very helpful to me over the years in a lot of my work.

Mary is now living at her ancestral home in Massachusetts. One significant aspect of the school is that they successfully made a transition to a new generation of teachers. This is often difficult when the strong founder of a school leaves. I think this is something that she really has to be proud of.

CPSIA information can be obtained
at www.ICGtesting.com
Printed in the USA
FSOW01n1921221117
41382FS

9 780986 016011